SURVIVING FADS, FASHION
&
FOLDEROL

Closing the We/They Gap

Charles Hughes Ph.D. & Steve Hance

CVR
Center for Values Research, Inc.
8848 Greenville Avenue
Dallas, Texas 75243-7143
(214) 553-8848
Fax (214) 553-9191
E-mail cvr@altinet.net
www.cvrdallas.com

Library of Congress Catalog
Card Number 98-70623

This book is dedicated to the memory of
Dr. Clare W. Graves. CVR was founded upon his model of
human behavior and values.

Charles L. Hughes, Ph.D.
President, CVR

Charles and Steve also express their appreciation to Suan,
Todd, Beverly, Tricia, Jay, Jeff and Rod for their contributions.

Table of Contents

Closing the We/They Gap   145

Final Comments   170

Terminology   171

About CVR   173

Preview

The purpose of this book is to show how the continuous onslaught of fads, fashion and folderol from alleged management experts is causing or maintaining a **gap between managers and the rest of the workforce.**

First: an analysis of **eight dimensions** of employee relations **where significant gaps** exist **between the attitudes of managers (We's) and non-managers (They's).**

Second: we will present an in-depth description of the dramatically disparate **Value Systems** dispersed among the **We's and They's.** This will explain why the gap exists. There exists among humans, significantly different ways of processing, interpreting and responding to communications — which are often ignored by managers.

Third: supporting the research are **quotations from employees** giving their reasons for their positive or negative attitudes. These quotations are taken from meetings with the CVR consulting staff in thousands of hours of **Attitude Survey Feedback Meetings** and private interviews.

Fourth: specific actions that either **close or open the We/They gap.**

Note: "Management" tends to be defined by employees as their immediate supervisor if the gap is narrow. If the gap is wide, management is "the boss's boss" — or higher in the organization.

The We/They Gap

Organizations experience difficulties created by the differences in the management thought process and the non-management thought process. The difference is an interruption in the continuity of the values, ideals, thinking and expectations of employee groups frequently called the **we/they gap**. It's an invisible opening creating an organizational barrier that can lead to failure of most initiatives.

The Center for Values Research, **CVR,** has 24 years of data from employee attitude survey research. The database includes over 1200 companies representing nearly one million employees. Through conducting survey feedback meetings **directly with employees,** eight primary areas of disparity between management and non-management employees have been identified. Using the **CVR Employee Attitude Survey,** individuals respond anonymously to each of the 20 attitude survey statements by indicating "*Agree, Disagree, or ?*"

The following chart is a summation of the database information. "Favorable response" is the percentage of employees in that group who responded favorably to the survey.

The We/They Gap Summary

Category	Favorable Management Responses	Favorable Non-management Responses	Percentage of Gap*
Trust among levels of hierarchy	66%	47%	19%
Freedom from retribution	81%	72%	9%
Communication and feedback on performance	65%	46%	19%
Cooperation among and within work groups	60%	48%	12%
Freedom from favoritism and discrimination	76%	51%	25%
A positive outlook on the future	67%	51%	16%
Opportunities to use skills and abilities	75%	62%	13%
Fair Compensation	65%	62%	3%**

* All differences are statistically significant at a .01 level.

**The scores in this category historically show over 30% difference. The gap has narrowed in the last five years due to a significant lowering of the management scores.

An Analysis of the Gap

Trust Among the Levels of Hierarchy

Managers are significantly more positive in their attitudes than the non-management employees are when it comes to trust. Management scores 66% favorable versus 47% favorable for the other employees. Management is more likely to trust each other than the workforce trusts management. From the CVR Employee Attitude Survey Feedback meetings with the "they's" we learned that they believe that managers will do anything to receive maximum financial rewards and personal gain. Expectations that are moving targets, unethical actions, legal violations and fad and flavor-of-the-month management styles all contribute to the erosion of trust. Management is sometimes known among the "they's" as the people with "flexible ethics." Non-management employees want to believe that managers will do the right thing (not just do things right) for the company and the employees. Their belief is that managers do the right thing only for themselves.

Freedom From Retribution

Managers are significantly more favorable than the other employees are when it comes to believing in freedom from retribution. Management scores 81% favorable versus a non-management score of 72% favorable. Not trusting that one can talk to the boss leads to fear of retribution. From the CVR Employee Attitude Survey Feedback meetings we learned that fear in the work place is common. A statement like "speak the truth and the truth will haunt you" is the pervasive belief among one fourth of the workforce. These employees see truth as unwanted by management. The party line, fad programs and management personnel view "best seller" catch phrases as the truth. Many times the reality of situations does not match the latest fashion in "manager-speak." Anyone not supporting the current, vogue idea is not viewed as a team player. Retribution is

4

believed to occur in many forms: lower raises, lack of opportunities, requests to "pursue other interests", being placed on special assignment, or any other feedback which creates belief that the truth is unwelcome or one will regret speaking candidly.

Communication and Feedback about Performance

Managers' attitudes are significantly more favorable than non-management employees are when it comes to communicating about performance. Management scores 65% favorable versus a non-management score of 46% favorable. From listening to thousands of employees discuss this topic in the survey feedback meetings comes the belief that management gives partial information, partial truths, irrelevant or late arriving information, changing expectations, floating quality standards and avoids the written documentation to support oral presentation of information. All contribute to the problem. This gap continues in spite of management's sincere efforts. With meeting after meeting, annual performance reviews and feedback, state of the business speeches, round table meetings, quarterly informational meetings, newsletters and numerous other tactics, the mysterious communication dilemma continues. There is an obvious Values System difference between the "we's" and the "they's" as to what is considered important in one's work life.

Cooperation Within and Among Work Groups and Teams

Managers' attitudes are significantly more favorable than the workforce when it comes to believing there is cooperation. Management scores 60% favorable versus a non-management score of 48% favorable. From asking specific questions, combined with careful listening in the extensive series of CVR Employee Attitude Survey Feedback meetings, most employees report they are satisfied with the cooperation they give one another within work groups and teams. Employees are frustrated when they do not see cooperation among managers. The gap is widened when a manager fosters competition among work groups instead of promoting cooperation. Managers marking their territory, inconsistent application of work rules, inconsistent standards regarding acceptable performance and a lack of resources to accomplish the job correctly all contribute to the problem. This is in spite of management initiatives towards team building, quality circles, 360 feedback, self-directed work teams, multi-culture diversity awareness, ISO certification, along with numerous other management tactics. The reason for the gap is that we are dealing with value systems that have dramatically different levels of awareness, therefore we find different attitudes and comprehension of the concept of "teams."

Freedom from Favoritism and Discrimination

Manager's attitudes are significantly more favorable than their employees are when it comes to seeing favoritism and discrimination. Management scores 76% favorable versus a non-management score of 51% favorable. Management believes that favoritism should nearly be gone considering government regulations and numerous union contracts that are in existence. None of these has eradicated favoritism. Many employees in the feedback meetings said favoritism is not a problem because they have learned to ignore or tolerate it and pretend it does not exist. Favoritism and discrimination continues to exist for many employees in hiring, bidding, bumping, promotions, inconsistent rule application, job assignments, overtime assignments and what constitutes acceptable behavior, just to name a few.

In meetings with management people about their results from the CVR Employee Attitude Survey, the majority believed that they are not involved in discriminatory practices or permitting favoritism to continue. Much of this stems from the fact that management develops the systems and procedures to benefit the corporation and consequently management, to the disadvantage of the "they's." This is a prime example of a value systems disparity in identifying the cause of discrimination.

Having a Positive Outlook for the Future

Managers are significantly more favorable than the employees they manage when it comes to seeing a favorable future. Management scores 67% favorable versus a non-management score of 51% favorable. Perhaps this is not surprising given the decade of downsizing, reengineering and restructuring. But the disparity of the understanding is significant and a mark on the reputation of the cost cutting consultants. Managers view a positive outlook for the future as financial and promotional opportunities. A few non-management employees may share these values. Most non-management employees view a positive outlook for the future as a cost of living raise coupled with getting into a preferred department, job and shift. Although employees may remain on the payroll following the implementation of a major "reduction in force" unanimously they will indicate that they "lost their job" even though they now work in another area until they can get "their job" back. When they see 40% to 60% of the new people coming in as temporaries from an agency, this further dims the view of the future.

Opportunities to Use Skills and Abilities

Managers' attitudes score significantly more favorable than non-management employees when it comes to seeing a favorable future. The national average scores 75% favorable for the "we's" versus 62% favorable for the "they's." In general, education is favored over experience. Experience has lost value and the addition of redundant, repetitive and non-value added responsibilities (e.g. long, incessant and useless meetings) all contribute to this gap. Employees were quite vocal in the CVR Employee Attitude Survey Feedback meetings that, when they can demonstrate competency and proficiency in job functions, they still are not given the freedom to perform to their fullest ability. This is quite contradictory to the assumption that empowerment leads to greater job satisfaction. Other feedback from the workforce dealt with suggestions encouraged but solutions rejected. Additionally, micro-managing, requirements to spend more time on paperwork than "doing the work", and adding computers to make work more efficient then "downsizing" as a result are all tactics which push people far outside of their comfort zones. Little wonder that change tends to be resisted.

Fair and Equitable Compensation

Managers are more favorable in their attitudes than non-management employees are when it comes to fair and equitable compensation. The national average scores 65% favorable for the "we's" versus 62% favorable for the "they's." This gap has closed significantly from 33% over the last five years due to a lowering of the favorable responses by the "we's." Money is one of the most emotionally charged topics in and out of industry. In the CVR Attitude Survey Feedback meetings, employees were quite pointed about their attitudes on pay. Fair pay was partially related to external equity in the market place, but more related to internal equity. Most serious among the grievances about fair pay was the retention of employees who do not meet performance standards. Granting of merit pay increases to an employee whom the peer group judged as doing poor quality work while a manager rated the performance higher leads to a serious disbelief that the system is fair. Major bonuses for management with minimal increases for the rest of the workforce, too much money in "at risk pay" and not in the base rate and, finally, secret pay survey data were reported in the meetings as the major sources of unfavorable attitudes. These are the consequence of the dramatic differences in value systems between compensation consultants who design pay systems and those who receive the pay.

The History of the We/They Gap

To understand the development of the gap within the work environment it is helpful to look at the origins of the gap. As far back as recorded history, the disparity among value systems of the "have's and have-not's" has led to conflict and misunderstanding. The most visible forms of disparate ways of thinking are seen in religious, cultural, government and societal norms. Each of these has been the cause of revolutions, wars, invasions, genocide and various other atrocities.

Religions

Within religions, many have ordained leaders as ministers, priests, rabbis, reverends, mullahs and other keepers of the faith who are set in the hierarchy above the faithful. The result has been the leaders determining what is the truth and placing the burden of abiding by the truth upon those followers. Throughout history new religious groups have developed when those led were looking for alternative leadership. When the religious values of the clergy came into conflict with the value systems of the laity the we/they gap opened up and the led sought new leaders. When laws and persecution made it difficult to find leaders with more compatible religious values, the "unfaithful" were exiled, ex-communicated or executed. But sometimes they escaped and sought new leadership or became leaders. The perpetuation of the gap was easy as long as the religion was in a language that few people understood. Once religion was written and spoken in a common language, some people began to think for themselves. Within today's world, sect leaders often talk in their esoteric language while the majority of converts listen with another language.

Missionaries covered the world to convert the "unenlightened." However, the "unenlightened" had a religion of their own which explained their world and helped them stay within their comfort

9

zone. The "unenlightened" did not believe they had a need for a new religion, but they were going to get one—like it or not—for their own good. Today these missionaries are called management consultants hired by the "we's" to convert the heathen "they's."

Royalty

Throughout most of history, there have been levels of hierarchy referred to as a class system. Among the "we's" there were the royalty, kings and czars and below them in the hierarchy were dukes, duchesses, earls, princes and princesses. At the lower levels of the hierarchy were the subjects, commoners and "the lower classes." The world has also experienced self-appointed royalty in the form of despots, tyrants and dictators with the next level of hierarchy being their minions. This continues in some Western countries today where there is yet no separation of church and state. Laws protecting realty (a word having the same root as "royalty") were historically sanctioned by the church. This limited the rights for private property for the masses. (One should never forget that the constitution made the United States the first country in history to have both separation of church and state and the right to have private property.) Royalty was held in high esteem (generally in their own minds) and exercised an inherited right to control their "subjects." Control took the form of taxation, servitude, police, convenient laws and fear of retribution for expressing objections to the hierarchy's policies. The subjects were kept in the equivalent of today's minimum wage poverty while the royalty could not comprehend why people were ungrateful. The result was insurrections, coups and other forms of rebellion or the intervention of a third party from another country. This continued until laws were introduced to reduce the we/they gap and bring about greater equality.

Today this model was and is reflective in American Industrial society until rebellion produced laws to protect the "they's" from the "we's." The National Labor Relations Act and the intervention of the labor union as a third party are just two examples.

Governments

The United States was created as a republic with a constitutional form of government and a few Western nations followed our lead. In its original form only "citizens", that is, the elite, educated and wealthy, elected the leadership of the United States. No one could vote unless you had property. All other males, all females, all blacks and Native Americans were disenfranchised. Thus, the United States began as a class-structured society but without the royalty. However, we created our own royalty known as the "robber barons" and industrialists who were unrestricted by laws to protect labor from exploitation. People in lower socioeconomic conditions believe that the economic system and taxation laws still favor those who are already well off.

Despite significant progress with the introduction of legislation to restrain the powerful, the we/they gaps still exist.

Corporations

Historically, the corporate hierarchical structure and means of control of the workforce has been derived from religions, republics, and the military. The we/they gap in companies has reflected the military concepts: officers and enlisted men, chain of command, duties, rules and regulations, perquisites for management, differing dress codes, separated dining facilities, amenities and the comfort of the working conditions. As with other hierarchy systems, exploitation is met with rebellion and third party intervention, expulsion or forced early retirement.

This is our legacy — we can learn from our history or live with the consequences of it.

A Perspective on Hierarchy

All organizations have a degree of hierarchy. Without hierarchy there is no organization, but simply chaos. This is true of the entire animal kingdom: lions and lawyers, monkeys and managers. It derives from power: physical and financial, nepotism and knowledge. Active entities arrange themselves into levels of influence and territorial command. A struggle for resources (human resources included) always results in an incessant rearrangement of the hierarchy.

There is no intention here to rearrange what appears to be a natural law, but rather to point out that **hierarchy does, in fact, exist**. The strategy is to deal with it as it is. The tactics are to **narrow the we/they gap** within the hierarchy for the benefit of all concerned.

VALUE SYSTEMS

There are many models of human development and psychology. Each one purports to be the ultimate model and proceeds to lay out a single dimensional view of human nature. Each of the varieties of human beings described, however, describes a different viewpoint and set of motivators, needs, wants and beliefs. Generally, the best selling books of the self-help or management fads describe the values of the author or a limited range of clientele. The next best seller does the same, but it is at odds with the one before. So, how do we find a true and universal description of human behavior and development that will hold up with different populations, ethnic groups, men and women, older and younger, Western and Eastern/Asian cultures? The answer is clear. There is **not** one form of human nature or psychology, but many. The search for the one and only view of humankind is simply a continuation of the ancient blind men and the elephant story (what is an elephant like depends on whom you ask). Most of the books on self-help and popular psychology about men's versus women's personalities are what statistician's call "sampling errors." A survey questionnaire by popular magazines does not tell us anything about men and women, but rather, the proclivities of a particular set of readers of that magazine who also enjoy psychobabble. The same narrow bias found in a best seller purporting to give the habits and principles of all effective adults based on "principles" derived from a particular religion. Nor can one easily comprehend the attitudes and values of blue-collar Americans from the speculation of a group of corporate executives who have never been to the shop floor or filled the role of a salaried and non-degreed support staff member. To find out what certain people or groups are like psychologically, one must inquire about that individual or particular set of people. In this section, we will build upon the work originated by Dr. Clare W. Graves and the continuous extension and additions to the database since 1974 by the Center for Values Research.

Deeper Than Attitudes

Attitudes are a response to a particular situation. Change the environment and you change the attitude. Positive attitudes occur when a person's deep-seated beliefs, motives, language and needs, i.e. **values**, are compatible with the environment in which the individual finds him or herself. Change the message, policy, practice, words, physical environment to match the values, and the attitude changes to a positive response. An attitude is a response to a situation. It is changeable whenever the situation changes. An attitude is a buffer between the situation and one's deepest beliefs, embedded in the language structure programmed into our psyche over many years of experiences. Values are the "why", not the what. Not what one is thinking, feeling, or doing but the deepest reasons beneath the surface. So values develop slowly and change slowly, if ever. Whereas attitudes can reverse from positive to negative or vice versa in a short period if the situation becomes more or less compatible with one's values. It is a question of fit or match. When behavior (what one is doing) is perfectly compatible with what one needs to do (values) a positive attitude results. Or at least for the moment. The situation changes and there may be a completely different attitude expressed or felt. If you want to change an attitude, change the situation because the deep-seated values will not change – or at least not easily or for along period of time.

In short, values are deep programming, complex, resistant to change except under certain stressful conditions we will explore later. Attitudes, behavior, feelings and thinking from moment to moment are adjustments to reduce tension between values and the situation, others, or culture. We will explore how values may, or may not, change later in our exploration. It is that simple. A positive attitude is the result of "having it your way." A negative attitude is when you have to "have it someone else's way."

Attitudes are therefore malleable, changeable and reflect the correlation of the situation with the individual's value system.

14

Values, conversely are deep psychologically programmed ways of interpreting the world, develop slowly, complexly and are resistant to change. Attitudes are temporal, changeable and a situational response. Once again, attitudes are a response to a particular situation, whereas values tend to be more constant regardless of the situation.

Levels of Awareness

Humans are aware of their own thinking, feeling and what they are doing, but in widely varying degrees. To assume every person is fully aware of feelings experienced is a frequent error. Relatively few people can trace the antecedents of a moment's surge of emotion. A highly aware individual may assume that everyone else has that capacity. When the best a person can say is, "I feel depressed", without a clue as to why, it simply means that particular individual has a low level of awareness. The reason for the emotion is lost in a large subconscious memory, if it were ever there in the first place. The function of psychotherapy is to provide the vocabulary necessary to raise the level of awareness so the feeling can be described and thus, controlled.

Relatively few people can retrace the memory flashes of events, visualizations, words, sounds, bodily states and smells and be instantaneously aware of the event or stimulus that triggered the chain of thoughts. Most are stuck with a thought, and clueless as how or why that idea came to consciousness. As with feelings, there are wide differences among individuals in the ability to connect the present with the past. They, too, are not in control of their inner feelings and thoughts and, therefore, are easily influenced and manipulated by others. They float in a timeless state of bewilderment about their thoughts, controlled by external forces, sometimes mystical, sometimes benevolent, sometimes malevolent.

Levels of awareness vary widely among individuals. For many, the ability to comprehend what one is doing at that moment is limited. Others can articulate thoughtfully and in detail why they are acting as they do at that moment. Whenever the awareness level is low, fabrication arises or acceptance of someone else's explanation for the behavior is uncritically accepted. This phenomenon frequently occurs in cults and in the implanting of false memories to young children and adults.

Levels of awareness (mindfulness) are a particular aspect of value systems and the stages of human psychological development. To understand other people it is imperative to remain aware that one's own level of awareness may be far greater than that of colleagues, spouses, children, friends and people about which one has had little direct experience (other cultures). The reverse is also true. Assumptions that everyone has developed the same degree of consciousness is naive and in personal transactions risky, if not dangerous.

Changing Values

The answer to the question "do values change?" is "it depends". If a person remains always in the same life-style situation, then values do not change because nothing else has changed. If the situation changes then values may change — albeit, slowly and almost imperceptibly. This process is a part of human psychological development. Some individuals or groups, however, become insulated or isolated from changes in the rest of the world. In that case, values will not change, but instead harden inside a protective comfort zone. In short, if nothing within the person's environment changes, then nothing about the person's values changes.

To use a computer analogy, values may change if the hardware is altered. Brain damage from strokes, trauma, surgery, tumors and psychoactive drugs may very well alter the value system permanently. Aside from severe "hardware damage", the more usual change in a value system is altering the programming of the computer-brain. Feedback that changes from the "usual" to the "unusual" and is sustained for long periods, will alter the programming, i.e. the system of thinking or values of the person being reprogrammed. For example, constant and consistent positive feedback, that is, positive from the perspective of the receiver, not sender, about one's behavior habituates that behavior and anchors the value system. Should there be a reversal of feedback from positive to constant negative, then eventually values will shift. In everyday life, however, we are receivers of a mixture of positive and negative feedback so little shift in values occurs. If we were to be subjected only to constant negative feedback in a hermetically sealed environment, cut off from everyone and everything except that which the programmers provide, values would be significantly reprogrammed in a matter of weeks. Examples are cults, military training and closed sect religions.

Intermittent and alternating feedback is our usual experience and that is the reason why efforts to reprogram employee thinking to conform to revisionist corporate culture visions and values are showing little success. Changing "corporate cultures" is often, in fact, the termination or silencing of those whose personal values conflict with the management version of "shared values." Politically, however, the citizens elect leaders who fit the voters shared values, rather than the citizens shifting to the elected politician's value systems. The difference is that in a democracy you change the leaders to get those whose perceived values correlate in relation to the majority of voters. Conversely, in a corporation, shareholders elect the leaders who in turn hire employees whose values may or may not fit the management values. Because of these changeable relationships, values of individual citizens and employees change little, or at least very gradually, over several years.

Reprogramming can occur whenever new behavior is mandatory. If individuals or groups are coerced, perhaps bribed, to engage in a dramatically new way, and escape is truly impossible, values

17

will yield to the new commands. Eventually behavior and values will match, unless the person escapes physically or mentally through total withdrawal, or in the extreme, suicide. Coercion will bring values into conformity, and the change will be painful mentally and physically.

The third way values can change is to reprogram the language the person uses. The value system **is** the language system. To say it another way, the language system constitutes the value system. The brain, to continue the computer metaphor, is a word processor and runs on a programming language just as a PC does. The computer program processes the content (data). The brain's processing program is language. If we were to learn a new language structure, new words and syntax, verb tense, we may have a new value system. When children learn two languages simultaneously, they can think in two languages with ease. As adults they have two memory systems and can access childhood events and emotions in both ways. On the other hand, when adults learn a second language, they have no childhood memory for events or emotions in the new language. These memories exist only in the original tongue. There may well be two disparate value systems operating in parallel, but without crossover. (This could be beneficial in dealing with painful negative memories. It is also useful when two adults learn a new language since it permits conversing about difficult topics, but without the childhood emotional garbage.)

New language, in the sense of new terminology, vogue words, language fads and fashion teach new values. Coded language in cliques, clubs, cults and corporations permit leaders to manipulate behavior. This is particularly true when new meanings are given to old words. This has the effect of cutting off communication with people outside the inner circle. It becomes easier to control and reprogram people's value systems.

This last point raises the question of should we attempt to reprogram people's values? If we start with the assumption that everyone seems to be trying to do it to each other at home, school, in political speeches, and in offices and factories, then the question is "are we aware of what is going on?" Whether the reprogramming of values is a ethical thing to do depends on the value system of the person asking the question, because it is usually the other person who is perceived in need of reprogramming, not oneself.

The Programming

Some behavior is hardwired, such as the operation of the autonomic nervous system, food processing, breathing and reflexes. The brain also is thought by some researchers to be hardwired for the acquisition of language. There may be other responses to the internal or external which do not require programming. These aspects of the brain architecture and neurological development are areas of intense research. For our purposes, the development of values is an acquired language process — a system of thinking.

Much of what people learn is simply by chance. Chance determines that some are born into a rich and enriched environment and others into a poor and impoverished home, if any. Some are big brother or sister; others are the younger brother or sister. Some experience an intact nuclear family with mother, father and perhaps grandparents. Some are born and reared by a single parent or surrogate in a child care facility. Some may experience mainstream Western religions; others experience alternative religions or none at all. Some grow up in peace, not war; plenty, not scarcity; strong, not weak; dark skinned, not light; robust, not sickly; educated, not illiterate; with a fully functioning brain, not a damaged one, and so on for the many variations of human existence. All of these apparently chance occurrences affect the shaping of value systems. The programming in the human computer-like brain system depends on the consequences of this complex variety of experiences. The consequences and outcomes create the programming process.

It is obvious that behaviors that result in positive outcomes will tend to repeat until it becomes a habit to act, think, and feel in a particular way. It is equally obvious that actions with negative outcomes will tend not to be repeated, at least after there is sufficient negative feedback. What is not so obvious is that what is positive to one person could be negative to another. This is overlooked in management, politics and adult relationships. Why should there not be a standard perception of positive and negative outcomes for all adults? Earlier experiences from infancy onward have laid down a foundation upon which value systems are constructed. The same behavior may have had radically different consequences for different people. That for which one child is rewarded, another is reprimanded — one praised, one punished. As was described in the preceding section, values may or may not change depending upon the consistency or inconsistency of the programming. This does not mean that early childhood programming absolutely determines adult values, but simply that they depend on the intensity and duration of repeated positive or negative consequences. It is a complex process.

Footnote: Avoidance of expected negative feedback automatically becomes a positive reinforcement. This apparent contradiction is due to the brain's electrochemical makeup. It is probably due to the adrenaline rush of fear. Whatever the true underlying brain process may be, this phenomenon is observed in people who repeatedly take risks. This raises serious issues for industrial safety, vehicle operation and other physical and mental activities. The near-miss accident, traffic violation, marginally legal or ethical acts must result in clear negative consequences from supervision, teachers, parents, religious authorities and law enforcement in order to prevent a repeat offense. The value conflicts within this last statement are pervasive.

Comment: Inconsistency in outcomes (positive versus negative feedback) results in a chaotic thought process, such as neurotic or psychotic behavior. What drives children, toddlers or teens "crazy" is inconsistency between, and within mother and father's rules and discipline. The same consequence will occur in industry and society at large resulting in anti-leadership and anti-social acts. Inconsistency scrambles the programming and contaminates the value system with dichotomies and conflicts, resulting in chaotic thinking, feeling and behavior. Consistency in feedback and communication is essential to the development of a coherent value system.

Comfort Zones

A comfort zone is both physical and mental. A physical comfort zone exists when there is no perceived danger to one's body, no pain and no tissue damage. A mental comfort zone exists when the person is at peace without fear or anxiety because values and behavior match. Whenever the basic values and beliefs are threatened by unusual feedback, people are forced out of their mental comfort zone. Just as seeing a threat of bodily harm is literally outside the physical comfort zone. The perimeter of the physical and mental comfort zones must be protected so one can remain inside and avoid threatening situations. "Do not go beyond the perimeter nor let anyone or anything inside!" The comfort zone provides a useful defense against bodily harm or the terror of ideas that are contrary to the value system. If actual behavior correlates with desired behavior then we have a comfortable condition. If another person imposes ideas or words and symbols which threaten values, discomfort results, and the remedy is to retreat into the comfort zone and shut off input and deny the existence of alternative views. The physical or mental size or intensity, so to speak, of comfort zones varies greatly among people depending upon the system of values and programming of the thought processes. To some, travel outside the country is outside their comfort zone, but to others, travel outside the county is a terrifying experience.

Sex, politics and religion are the most likely areas for comfort zone issues since these values are often deeply programmed into childhood memories before analytic thinking was possible.

Forbidden sounds, words spoken, results in a retreat to the silence of the comfort zone. Forbidden sights provoke a return to the blindness in the comfort zone. One's own acts that are contrary to one's values permit negative memories to fade away.

Values will not change if one remains exclusively within the comfort zone. If there is positive feedback only, in which personal values and the values of others are perfectly matched, awareness of the world will be forever limited. Values do not change when everything correlates one-to-one. For values to change, not that they should, one has to get outside the comfort zone, that is, to experience unfamiliar feedback. When new and unusual situations and people catch a person outside the comfort zone, the negative feedback raises consciousness. However, too little movement outside the comfort zone results in no change of awareness. (Return to the safe zone, and try not to be caught out there again!) Zero change results. Oppositely, too much, too far, too fast of a change and the values may be shattered and prevent return to the safety of the comfort zone. The basic values programs have been corrupted and may cause the person's programming to "crash". The size of the comfort zone must be considered when giving or receiving feedback. Strongly discomforting situations may produce negative and destructive changes. A moderate amount of negative feedback can produce positive changes in thinking, feeling and behavior — but how does one know the size of the comfort zone and when enough is the right amount? As we develop the value systems model, the answer will become clearer.

See no evil, hear no evil, speak no evil – learn nothing.

Values: Systems of Thinking

As was introduced earlier, people vary significantly in their levels of awareness and degrees of consciousness. With some systems of thinking the awareness is limited to such an extent that thoughts are attributed to spirits and gods. Needs, wants and motives are believed to come from outside and thus not under self-control, consequently there is no personal responsibility for the consequences of behavior. Literally believing "the devil made me do it", or "it was a voice from a god". The individual is without individuality–a pawn in a cosmic chess game. One system of thinking (values) places the individual as the controller of everything–a demigod at the center of the universe, with a ruthless disregard for the consequences. Other value systems range between these extremes. One person's level of awareness may be radically different from another's.

Language is the key to consciousness. Language is the process by which humans interpret events. Language **is** the value system. A value system **is** the use of language. As we develop the model, be mindful of one's and others use of words. This is the key to understanding values.

Dimensions of Values

We will explore values and their development with these dimensions:

Source: From where did this particular value system originate?

Needs: What are the unquestioned ideas programmed deeply into one's language?

Wants: What motives and desires operate at a superficial level?

Life and Death: What do these ideas mean and what are the consequences?

Time and Space: Is the focus on past, present or future — expansive or constricted?

Love and Hate: What attracts and what repels — who is trusted and who is feared?

Content and Process: How does learning occur?

Language: What communication styles are characteristic of the value system?

Work: Which job is satisfying and why?

Few individuals have a single set of values equally strong for all of these dimensions. Most people are mixtures and may hold different values on different aspects of life. People operating within their comfort zones have strong "primary" values coupled with a less strong "secondary" set of beliefs. For purposes of communication and clarity, **value systems will be described in their purest form.**

System 1 – Conditioned

The first system of values is the absence of values. The infant is born without language and without conscious thinking and, therefore, values are absent. As language develops, values develop. Initially the child operates on hardwired responses built into the brain schema by DNA. The brainstem controls the autonomic functions of respiration, food processing and other vital bodily functions. Soon the limbic system produces emotional responses to internal and external stimuli, but without nouns with which to label the chemical changes underlying emotions, there is not a glimmer of awareness. This is a natural initial condition, except for infants born with brain defects or who experience severe trauma and/or neglect. Fortunately, in nearly all cases the child can process the stimuli and learn conditioned responses. System 1 — Conditioned — is identified in the model to emphasize that this is where all humans began their development and where some shall return if forced far out of their comfort zone, as in "post-traumatic shock syndrome."

The process of development beyond System 1 begins with the acquisition of language. Children are born with the ability to learn language, beginning the vowel sounds characteristic of their culture. They practice the sounds until they match those of the person teaching. Consonants begin to be learned within the set available in that language, whether tonal or atonal. Combinations of vocalized sounds come next. Then nouns are acquired since they name concrete, visible, tangible and tastable objects. Verbs are learned to name the visible actions of nouns. Later the nouns are enriched through the addition of adjectives. Then adverbs to enrich the verbs. Somewhere in the process the concept of "self", the "me" or "I" (or the child's name) develops and the true consciousness arises and permits a development of the next value system.

System 2 – Clannish

Source: Tribalistic values are learned from a narrow range of sources within a relatively small physical and mental comfort zone. Among these sources are group-focused activities, such as family events, peers at school, the neighborhood gang, rites of initiation, sports teams, religious ceremonies or later, military basic training. Of particular importance are the values expressed and promulgated by the leader of the "tribe" — the chieftain, the coach, the parent, older sibling or anyone in a clear position of power. The chieftain not only prescribes what the group does and says, but also proscribes what is out of bounds and forbidden behavior and speech. In this tightly controlled and not necessarily benevolent environment, the programming of values is constant and relentless. The clan's bonds among its members are strengthened through rituals. Rituals are repeated frequently, but have no intrinsic meaning. Rituals are the means of keeping the members of the tribe inside the clan's comfort zone. Group rituals, with this process of bonding, are repetitious. Displaying the clan's symbols (fetishes, flags, dress codes, totems, logos etc.), coupled with repetitive group activities (songs, prayers, dances, chants, feasts, etc.) serves to teach a clannish value system.

By these means, System 2 values are implanted and imbedded permanently into thought processes and personal identity. Storytellers who pass on the oral traditions of the clan, its history, its conflicts with other tribes, the Patriarchal or Matriarchal lineage, its heroes and heroines and its secrets, give strength to the members through the power of the tribe. The clan's shaman (witchdoctor, medicine man) brings the mystery necessary to hold the clan together and to banish evil spirits from body and soul. The shaman never shares secrets with the clan, or even the chieftain, for doing so would destroy the magic and cause the witchdoctor's powers to disappear. Totems are worshiped as symbols of deceased elders or idols of tribal gods. Taboos are words never to speak lest the clan be destroyed by evil forces or acts which are forbidden.

26

In the industrial scene, these clannish values are the "corporate culture." When the high chieftains, (management) attempt to change the corporate cultural values rapidly, the clannishness of the workforce exerts group-based resistance or seeks new chieftains — the labor union. This is most noticeable when the old cultural comfort zone perimeter has been penetrated by a series of come-and-go managers, each with a short-lived fad, fashion or folderol.

Culturally, clannish values appear as ethnocentric identities, religion, race and ancestry. Coercive political regimes force clashes among ancient cultures. Ethnic war "cleansing" results in brutal tribal warfare without remorse. Extreme coercion under dictatorships does not result in loss of ethnic or national identities any more than the forbidding of worship eradicates religious values. There are many other examples historically and currently.

Needs: The tribal members share a deeply felt need for physical security. In the workplace, safety and freedom from bodily harm are paramount, for it is physical skills that are the primary means of income. Losing the use of hands and/or limbs means "out-of-work," perhaps permanently. Freedom from attack by other tribes requires constant vigilance. It is the role of the chieftain to organize protection of the perimeter of the tribal territory. Psychological safety is an equally strong need, for the comfort zone in System 2 is small. It is the role of the shaman or witchdoctor to provide protection from or removal of evil spells. Mysterious and frightening signs and symbols raise fear of mental and physical invasion and control. Strange new sounds of unknown words ("empowerment") are understood only within existing vocabulary ("entitlement"). Insecurity with management fads is particularly heightened when the deliverer of the message is anyone other than the immediate leader of the clan. Pronouncements from executives and imposition of strange terminology by consultants produce a withdrawal to a mental place far inside the comfort zone. Impersonal media in the form of videos with an unknown "talking head" do little to communicate. The media, which can effectively communicate the message, are respected leaders/chieftains. A leader who gives constant reassurance that all is well and takes personal responsibility for anything new is more likely to get positive change — though it will be quite slow (months and years, not days and weeks). Therefore, when the environment, both physical and mental, remains stable, System 2 is not alarmed by the threat of being moved too far or too fast outside the comfort zone. While it is out of fashion in management and social psychology, traditional benevolent protection is what the clan desires.

Wants: People with strong primary or secondary System 2 values truly want to serve the chieftain. The head of the clan, the father or grandmother, the supervisor, is the beginning and end of the leadership hierarchy, although charismatic higher level leaders may serve in a figurehead god-like role. Surprise invasions by outsiders or "wandering about" by high level "super-chieftains" without the immediate chieftain's knowledge and pre-notification of the tribe are not seen as friendly interest, but rather a potential for criticism and dispensing of wrath.

Within the clan age is respected, or its industrial equivalent, seniority. The leader of the clan would be well served if he or she were older in age or service, or preferably both. Our research has found great resentment when younger supervisors who are also outsiders are appointed chieftain. Since from ages ago chieftains have generally been male, it is more difficult for a female. Patriarchy, with all the controversy swirling around it, is a historical fact but obviously **not** a reason to avoid placing females in charge of tribal groups, for the tribe respects competence and experience.

Another powerful "want" is the opportunity to participate in rituals — repetitive and predictable actions that bond the members together and create the group comfort zone. Religions provide ritualistic opportunities which give uniqueness and a sense of being part of something greater than oneself, whether a small worshipful group or a larger institution. Within our everyday environment, regular, brief and frequent huddles by the tribe create a bond. The same applies to larger institutional gatherings. This includes sports gathering of fans that share in their team's victories or defeats, clannish symbols, cheers and sometimes violence against the members of the opposition. In the clannish system of thinking, eating together is essential to the bonding ritual, with members of the clan taking turns providing the food offering. The same can be true in families when meals are taken together, with certain ritualistic patterns and prayers repeatedly anchoring positive memories.

In a clan, with its inherent hierarchy of power, age and knowledge, it is wise to know one's place. Overstepping the unmarked boundaries between "me and thee" could be dangerous, for there is a rigidly structured and enforced hierarchy. Younger members of the tribe learn from negative feedback where they fit in the system and thus the clan maintains its integrity and identity for generations. Position in the ranking is identified by symbols: uniform, vestment, miter, crown, scepter, flag, medallion, title, tattoo, throne, pay grade and speech pattern.

The objective of the hierarchical arrangement, with all its rituals and regalia, is to provide safety within the comfort zone by blending into the group, but always in accordance with one's clearly defined role. However, from the apparent rigidity and control also comes a form of personal power by being a member of a cohesive, all-for-one-and-one-for-all group, gang or team with presumed invincibility.

Life and Death: To live and to die is a natural and cyclical event. One is born and then one dies and that is the way things are. Life this time around is merely a manifestation of the wheel of life as the spirit recycles once more, now and forever. Reincarnation is a spiritual concept important to the eternal continuation of the tribe's existence. One's own death is less

29

important than perpetuating the clan's beliefs, for they represent the universality of spirit. If the family name and history lives on throughout a succession of generations, then the mission is accomplished. This manifests itself as self-sacrificing patriotism, tracing the roots of family trees, racial pride and ethnocentrism, not to mention continuity through incorporation.

In this polytheistic universe, omniscient, all powerful and ever-present gods control everything and everyone — all actions, motives, outcomes and environmental events. Motives are not believed to originate in one's brain, but rather in the mind of one of the many benevolent or malevolent gods. Spontaneous, original and creative thoughts are attributed to one of the plethora of immortal gods intervening in human affairs. If mortals are exempted from being the creator, they are relieved of responsibility for their own condition, whether it is benign or malignant, oppressed or oppressor, victim or persecutor — it is merely a god's will being done. This provides a comforting view of life and death, which maintains the System 2 self-concept.

Time and Space: When the future is assured by unquestioned and unswerving faith, then there is no essential need to look too far ahead in time — a few days or weeks is sufficient. When the past extends to the beginning of time at the creation of the earth, the genesis of the clan is time zero. The past verb tense is the same as the future verb tense. In supremely tribalistic cultures, the language has only the present tense. In this particular way of viewing the world as unchanging and human nature immutable, the past goes far, far back and the future will soon arrive. The most important time, however, is now. Relishing the immediacy of the moment without being bound by an artificial construct of "time" permits spontaneity of action (so long as it is within the comfort zone). Reenactments of age old and unchanging rituals merges the past into the present and forecloses much thought about the future.

Love and Hate: Blood relatives come first and relations by marriage come a distant second, literally relatives "in law" only.

Love is expressed for "kinfolk" regardless of their transgressions. In some clans created by the banding together of several individuals who have been rejected or ejected by the family, a form of "blood-by-bonding" is created. Non-relatives who are not genetic siblings become "blood brothers" and "blood sisters" and are accorded all the privileges and protection the created clan has to give. Blood is truly thicker than water. However, men and women's tribes engage in gender warfare.

The family-first focus also permits and encourages hate toward other clans. In its extreme, the tribal warfare and reciprocal revenge cycle begins for some real or imagined offense and "ethnic cleansing" results, whether in the Americas, Europe, Asia, Africa or our inner-city ghettos. All tribes consider themselves "the people", that is the "chosen" clan, and other tribes, in their view, are "sub-humans" who have no right to exist. Annihilation may not be literal, but rather, enslavement and segregation.

System 2 thinking loves old things, old ideas, old people and old ways, because the past is remembered as though it were recent. Efforts to get the clan members to let go of the past is understood as expecting them to erase their history. If one has to cut the roots, how does the family tree grow? Others often interpret this resistance, managers included, as stubbornness when in fact it is fear of loss of identity. Oldness is inside the comfort zone and newness is anything outside of it. Newness is hated, i.e. feared. New ways of working with new systems and machines imposed in a rush to revolutionize the production system to corporate competitive advantage have been met with employee solidarity in the sisterhood and brotherhood of unions.

Content and Process: The process by which information is acquired in System 2 thinking is gradual, incremental small bites of ideas (content) taught orally by the elders, shamans and leaders. The information must be connected to the past and be presented as simply a continuation of the ways things have always been done. Attempts at quantum change are useless. For effective change, it is necessary to start early and go slowly. Instant feedback about performance for each segment of the content anchors the information and closes the loop of communication. The attention span will be relatively short unless there is clear connection between the new information and the existing situation. As with all value systems, it is essential to consider the vocabulary and language style most compatible with the mental comfort zone.

Language: To understand and communicate with people strong in System 2 values it is mandatory that one acquire a working knowledge of the tribes accepted vocabulary, as is also true when dealing with people who speak and think in a different language. Beyond the language barrier of native tongues there is still the barrier within spoken English and an even more serious gap with the printed word. While this is true for all value systems, the clannish system of thinking uses only a fraction of the quarter million plus words in English. In a relatively small comfort zone, compared to other value systems, words take on concrete meaning. Abstract ideas are not a part of the thought or memory process. Every thought, figure of speech, belief, spirit and god has a tangible existence. Every message from trusted leaders is taken literally, without nuance or reinterpretation. The usual consequences of misunderstanding are severe and are observed today in politics, international relations and employee and domestic relations.

Operating within the clan's vocabulary, idioms and slang, assuming they are used properly, contributes to communication effectiveness. The dictionary definition may not reflect the subtlety nor reflect the context in which the term is used. It is, rather, the semantics — the reaction to a word or sign — that is the key to communication with all value systems, especially Clannish.

Repetitious phrases are a clannish custom by which clarity of meaning is assured. Not fully understanding the leader's wishes could lead to disapproval or error, and the thought of the potential of ensuing wrath is terrifying. Effective communication requires redundancy. Wanting to please the leader is indicated by placing a "?" at the end of what is otherwise a declarative sentence. This approval seeking tone is referred to as "up talk," (a characteristic of the early-teens group still in their tribal clan mode.) With the need for redundancy and the tradition of oral rather than written communication, it is characteristic of System 2 to have run-on dialogues, in other words, non-stop, simultaneous and overlapping conversations. However, when all the talking is done, it is still the chieftain who gets the last word and makes the decision. System 2 is not comfortable with open participative democracy or unrestricted and leaderless employee involvement.

Work: Clannish values are the primary or secondary pattern for about 25% of the workforce and found in lesser skilled and lower paying job classifications. Highest in work satisfaction are jobs that are repetitive and routine. Decision-making is left to the leader. Activities that require rhythmic physical movement or are machine paced fulfill this need, as are jobs in which several people act in tandem in a true team fashion. Singing and dancing accompanied by patterned arm movements is a part of the clan's bonding process and should be a part of the tribal huddles. Many people who are otherwise not strong in System 2 values express off-the-job tribalism in this manner.

Group contact is highly compatible, comforting and appropriate with teamwork a natural style. No need for team building, as long as there is appropriate team leadership.

Summary of System 2 – Clannish Values: The key to understanding is to know the tribe and the chieftain's values. Respect for the clan's rituals and myths is essential. Safety and security are very important. Little self-awareness is needed for identity comes from the family, including the work family.

System 3 – Cynical

Source: Egocentrism replaces tribalism when invasion by another clan drives the clan out of its comfort zone. The ensuing dissonance causes conflict in thinking when the new chieftain imposes radical ideas and destroys the totems. Being captured or merging with a group with different clannish concepts takes the tribe far enough out of the comfort zone to produce a basic values shift. While the process takes months of anguish, insight into "outsider's" ways eventually gives rise to a new level of awareness. However, the awareness is that one is alone with no protective clan with which to huddle, no benevolent leader and no fixed world of comforting beliefs. The aloneness places the person at the center of a universe in which one is his or her own god.

Cynical persons place an extremely high value on their own thoughts. They operate in an endless loop of ideas, each reinforcing the other with little external input. Largely, this circular thought process precludes influence by others, for contrary beliefs are met with cynicism and protective bluster. In spite of such bravado, their comfort zone is really rather small and lonely. The perimeter is fiercely guarded in the manner of The Wizard of Oz behind the curtain bellowing bombastically to frighten Dorothy and her entourage.

Chieftains, elders, family, parents and supervisors are rejected in favor of being the master or mistress of one's own destiny and god of a tiny universe. Former leaders are challenged or killed (literally or figuratively) if they resist. The goal of the egocentric is to become the tribal leader and turn the clan into a gang of loyal and obedient servants willing to destroy whatever or whomever, as ordered. Ancient and comforting clan rituals are replaced with new self-centered rituals as a technique of controlling the tribe. Added to the cynical manipulation is physical force, whether it is muscle power, mechanical power, firepower or horsepower.

Totems and taboos of the old tribe are inverted as an expression of cynicism and rejection so that which was worshipped is now despised. Taboos are deliberately violated and idols (both godly and human) are destroyed. Extremism reigns in both thought and action, and terrorism is an instrument of subjugation of all who resist.

Needs: In spite of a hard surfaced exterior shell, inside the egocentric fears death. To conquer death would be the ultimate ego-trip thus there is a strong need to look death in the face through tests of physical danger. To suffer injury in a near-death act and yet survive is proof to the cynic of invincibility, and it gives a chance for exhibitionism. In addition to physical danger, System 3 thinking demands psychological risk particularly in the use of psychoactive drugs. To conquer and control drugs when lesser persons cannot do so would be proof of superman or superwoman invincibility. Not believing addiction is possible for them they think it is only the weak who succumb ("I can quit anytime I want").

A contingent need is constant challenge, and here is where System 3 values occasionally make breakthroughs where others of a more rational nature would quit. However, that may be a positive virtue to society only in the intellectual realm. Being a physically oriented individual, extreme sports are a more common expression and are seen as virtues by other egocentrics. The need for challenge leads to behavior that is disruptive. The advantage of initiating a disruption in the environment is the opportunity to seize control of others while they are disoriented and confused. The need to take charge sometimes results in saving others, but only until the command position is secured. Malevolent exploitation will follow.

Wants: The desire to dominate others leads to confrontation with people with power. In the process of confronting and controlling another dominant person feeds the ego. Controlling persons of lesser power is not a challenge for the egocentric already "owns" them. Confrontational challenges serve to

35

establish who is "alpha male" or "alpha female." As a result of winning the power contest, the individual can now afford to be alone for awhile building strength for the next fight. Inevitably, another System 3 person challenges the cynic's position in the power structure, then the process repeats. Challenges are not limited to the physical struggle, but also verbal abuse, with words and "nastygrams" being thrown back and forth like sticks and stones. Shouting matches, often laced with profanities and a plethora of "four-letter words" are part of the harassment and intimidation process. The diatribe escalates until someone runs out of mental energy or a third party intervenes. The objective of the contest is to take another's place in the hierarchy. With control of the loser's belongings, territory and tribe, the egocentric is now free to exploit the assets and bully the people into a gang of obedient blind-faith followers.

Life and Death: Death is feared, although the need for physical danger may seemingly contradict that idea. Challenging death and surviving proves toughness. However, what happens when a supremely self-centered person does die? The answer is "the end of everything!" meaning if everything revolves around the god-like "center of the universe" then everything and everyone else simply ceases to exist also. When the self-anointed creator dies, nothing can remain. So to make sure there is no continued existence beyond oneself System 3 may destroy everything and everyone on the way to his or her death. The cynic believes that God is already dead and "I'm still alive" — the ultimate egoism. The nihilist believes in the total disregard of laws and total and absolute destructiveness —including oneself.

Time and Space: The past is a short time frame; the future is near-term also. If one is god-like then time is of no concern — a characteristic that causes cynics to repeat the same mistakes and not to learn very much from experience. Recidivism of antisocial behavior often leads to repeated illegal and physically violent offenses and incarceration. Violation of company policies against sexual or other harassment occurs, in spite of stern warnings or disciplinary actions. When termination of employment occurs, innocence is proclaimed and followed by threats of lawsuits or bodily harm. In the drive to "live for now and to hell with tomorrow!" others are trampled.

The only space that matters to System 3 is the space occupied by the egocentric. Outside the immediate area, there is nothing of importance. Otherwise if it were important it would be nearby orbiting "the center of the universe."

Love and Hate: The word "love" may be inappropriate, for if there is any form of love it is self-love, and even that is transparently shallow. "Tough Love" has been introduced into our culture, but the behavior is still brutal terrorism. "Love" from a System 3 values perspective is a guise for imminent aggression or rejection. It is as if love is expressed as a connived means of lifting someone up in order to drop him or her as soon as the person becomes trusting and vulnerable.

Challengers to the cynic's power are hated enough to be destroyed mentally and/or physically. Being the challenger is one thing, but being challenged is another. Power is what egocentrics love, especially power over others to engage in obsequious behavior, which passes for a form of love (sex). A tribal person who has accepted the egocentric as a chieftain will tolerate abuse in a distortion of love. To an egocentric, male or female, the other person "asked for it", thus reversing the roles of perpetrator and victim. The hatred of egocentric males for women and egocentric females for men is acted out in verbal or physical sexual aggression. The need to dominate sexually may extend to male vs. male and female vs. female aggression.

Content and Process: The short view of time requires that communications be quick, direct and delivered in short bursts. The system of thinking and programming is not linear, so disconnected information is effective, as long as one tests that the message was received by asking it to be repeated back. Unique to this value system, it is mandatory that the "do-not-do's" are communicated in advance of the "do's," rather than the usual sequence of feedback after an error. Feedforward, so to speak, of what is to be avoided. Feedback after the error is essentially too late to change the already-acted-out behavior. If one is to be a god, then feedback from lesser mortals is to be avoided, for who are they to judge? All of these tendencies lead to an erratic attention span, unless the topic is "I."

Language: The vocabulary employed by egocentric males is "macho" or for the female egocentric, "macha," so to speak. In both instances, it is aggressive, cynical and snide as if sneering at the listener. A tinge of wariness and guarded suspicion is in the tone, and even when on best behavior, it sounds like a lie (and probably it is.) The negative, aggressive tone forebodes the negative, aggressive action that is likely to follow. If System 3 is displeased when his or her demands are not met quickly, attack will follow. When the transaction is over, there is usually abrupt closure, assuming he or she got what was wanted. Otherwise, the hostility will escalate, unless the other person stands ground, remains calm and shows no weakness. In spite of the outcome of the contest of willpower, egocentrics always try to get the last word.

Work: System 3 is the primary or secondary pattern for about 5% of the workforce and working in short term employment situations. Physically difficult work is appealing for it gives an opportunity to display strength and toughness of mind and body. However, this also poses a safety risk. If the job is isolated, there must be someone in control. Work with a short cycle time to match the short attention span is most compatible, especially if machine paced. Otherwise the "boss" will have to set the pace and "run the crew" to prevent loitering or malingering. On-the-job-training is appropriate, since classroom training will be disruptive and it also lacks the intense personal attention necessary to impart the necessary skills.

Summary of System 3 – Cynical Values: Rugged individualism is expressed through power and force. Life experiences have taught the value of being anti-social. Being suspicious of others' motives has served well in avoiding exploitation by people with power. Struggling for survival has been necessary since childhood. Exploiting people before being exploited by them is an ingrained habit. In short, life is a fight.

System 4 — Conventional

Source: Conformist values develop when cynics are forced sufficiently far out of their comfort zone. The awareness that both the weak and the strong die is often the catalyst. The search for a reason for one's miserable existence becomes a consuming passion. The exploration of wider ranges of ideas and a more comprehensive understanding of how things work begins the building of a highly elaborate structure of beliefs. This wide-range knowledge of the things beyond one's selfish ego creates a systematic, rather than chaotic, worldview.

The most important sources of conventional thinking are values from institutionalized sources: religions and their Holy Scriptures, governments and their statutory laws, militaries and their rules and regulations, and corporations and their policies. Also emanating from these institutional sources are formalities of codified behavior. Correctness in speech, behavior, thinking, attire, decorum and etiquette are learned as prearranged codes of conduct. For each particular life situation, the codes serve to standardize relationships with humans—and God. Recorded history is the guiding principle, for with the advent of this value system, literacy is mandatory. The printed word is authoritative, inviolate and inerrant. The rule of law replaces rule by humans. Abstract concepts are now possible and scientific literacy is gained, although some laws of physics and biology conflict with religious beliefs. System 4 thinking avoids the conflict between religion and science through hermetically sealed separate compartments. Right and wrong, morality and immorality and binary thinking provide stability to life. The comfort zone is enlarged, but the perimeter is well fortified.

Contrary to the assumptions of humanistic movements, New Age theorists and popular Human Resource gurus, this value system is alive, well and flourishing — and that is probably the good news for a sane society. Data gathered by CVR (Center for Values Research) confirms that the "Silent Majority" did not fade away, but simply went silent until the fads, fashion and folderol proved to be faulty and not appropriate for all occasions.

Needs: An all-encompassing well-engineered structure of unyielding ethical principles, non-compromised commandments and rigid rules and regulations fulfill the need for a guidance system. Life is made less tedious if there are predictable responses for each possible situation, as well as certainty of behavior. Gaining control over the universe and one's own urges makes it possible to remain comfortably inside the enclave of the comfort zone. Closing all the loops, completing all assigned tasks and fulfilling one's duties is essential before relaxation is permissible. "Business before pleasure." "Laundry before love."

Everything in its place and a place for everything. Neatness and orderliness of objects — and people — provides a supportive infrastructure of reliable efficiency. Do things right the first time and do not waste time, money and energy. These attributes are compatible with a wide range of work and home situations. However, since things do not always go according to plan, contingency backups are always available for rescue and have already been contrived and tested.

Wants: Conforming to the accepted norms of the majority, or to the powerful people in charge of the system, permits one to be a "good person." Acting in accordance with these expected patterns demonstrates to the powerful and to oneself that "I am a good person by virtue of my good deeds." Remaining, thus, within the perimeters of the comfort zone, negative feedback or punishment is avoided. Wanting to be perfect and expecting all others to strive for perfection is a prime motivator. The difficulty in extreme System 4 thinking is the virtual impossibility of achieving human perfection, although perfectibility is worshiped in an idealized person. In the absence perfection, feelings of guilt (sin) result, along with other forms of self-punishment. Salvation for sin may be sought through religions that advocate mortification of the flesh, or at least the seeking of redemption through penance. Absolution for transgressions is resolved by

41

remorseful confession of imperfection and requests for redemption through grace.

Perfection in others is also expected and imperfection is to be punished. Collective guilt becomes a control mechanism for the more powerful over the lesser. Guilt inducing oration invoking the fear of hellfire and eternal damnation can induce millions to sacrifice the lives of others who do not repent the sins they did not even know they had committed.

Life and Death: With a focus on "there and then" more than "here and now", it is easy in System 4 thinking to delay one's rewards and punishments until an afterlife. Come the ultimate judgment day, however, accounts must be settled. The balance of good deeds and evil acts is calculated and the consequences enjoyed or suffered depending on the ratio of one to the other. At the day of reckoning, if one has conformed during natural life, body and soul will be reunited. There are obvious parallels in corporate life: judgment of work performed while employed, and the after-work-life of a comfortable retirement or involuntary termination.

With the immense ability and skill to delay consequences, persons with this conventional thought process exhibit tremendous patience. Believing that crime is followed by punishment, ultimately universal justice will prevail. Even when one dies, that is of lesser importance so long as the cherished institutions live on. Not just religious institutions, but nations and corporations must outlive individuals. In this way, the values represented by System 4 are perpetuated — and that is the source of true faith.

Time and Space: With the comforting perspective of history and the belief in the inevitable, time becomes a linear, regular and calibrated process. The past determines the future with little variance from the predetermined trajectory. Events of history forecast the future and foreclose efforts to redirect events. It is now as it was then and forever shall be. Change is therefore difficult to imagine if it is quantum, but feasible if it is incremental. Change occurs, yet ever so slowly and almost imperceptibly. There exists a linear cause and effect relationship of what was "then" must be "now" and "thence."

With the comprehensive ability to deal with abstractions and intricately constructed concepts comes an expanded relationship with space. Not just the cosmos, but space in an everyday configuration of highways, buildings, subatomic particles and three dimensional representations, thus making possible science and engineering to conquer, control and predict the world. However, with this capacity comes compartmentalization of ideas, beliefs and a relative lack of concern for things and people outside that compartment.

Love and Hate: When there is a strong and highly integrated thought process of morality versus immorality and a belief in the one true set of values, it is easy to love others whose concepts correlate. Love derives from sharing the same comfort zone. Love becomes, in part, the predictability of another's responses. A way of loving oneself is to find others, who love the same ideas, share the same values and judge others by the same set of criteria. The group who loves one another for their sameness can also hate non-believers for their differentness. Confrontation with those who believe differently results in hate (actually fear), for in the interaction beliefs may be challenged and shaken. To avoid the uneasiness of doubt it is necessary to hate those who believe differently as "believing nothing at all" (infidels.) In extreme, System 4 rigidity results in religious crusades, inquisitions and vengeance.

Traditions give comfort and reliability. Love for cultural, corporate and family traditions provide a structure for freedom from fear. Traditions are living proof that certain principles prevail and perpetuate the order of the universe. Change for what is perceived as change for the sake of change is resisted. "If it has worked for this long, why make a change now and risk disaster?" "If it ain't busted, don't fix it."

43

Radical, vogue, new and unproven styles and methods are to be avoided. Resistance to fad, fashion and folderol is at its zenith with System 4's conventional thinking. Conventional values means waiting until something is proven to be of good design, good reliability and absolute perfection before wasting time, talent, energy and money. System 4 is not a risk-taking process, and people with these values "make haste slowly." Leaders who are conscious of this way of thinking have learned to "start early, go slowly" when making change.

Content and Process: With a highly structured system of thinking comes an immense capacity to learn large amounts of information, categorized and placed into memory (provided the data is acquired sequentially.) Random inputs to the highly programmed mental computer are perceived as chaotic and without orderliness or predictability. Learning, therefore, is linear with a detailed agenda leading to logical conclusions. While feedback about the correctness of what is being learned can be delayed (patience and perseverance), extended "feedforward" (opposite of feedback) is required so that the final result will be judged as logical. Accompanying this capacity is an attention span of hours, days and even years. This ability correlates with the view of time as having a long past and a long future.

Language: Conventional values require conventional vocabularies. The "received" language characteristic of the mainstream culture forms the approved model of usage and therefore, thinking. Native speakers of a particular language who stay within the mainstream vocabulary accepted by tradition as correct easily conform to the values inherent in the nouns, verbs, adjectives and adverbs. Whereas, Clannish cultures may limit verbs to the present tense. In Conventional cultures the verbs tenses include past, present and future. Sureness of beliefs is evidenced by the frequent use of declarative sentences, as opposed to conditional sentences. Judgmental words ("should, ought to, got to") are frequent and digital ("yes", "no"; "right", "wrong") terms express the belief in an objective set of values external to human beings.

Reasoning is based on cause and effect using deductive (as opposed to inductive) rules of logic. Syllogisms ("all A is C: all B is A, therefore all B is C") give airtight logic, if one accepts the premises. "X (faith based assumption) **is**, and Y (correlated assumption) **is, therefore,** Z is absolutely true.

A characteristic of the System 4 thought process is a superior, righteous tone of voice driven by absolute conviction of the rightness of one's belief. Closure on a topic of concern or dialog is achieved when that which set forth to be proved, has been logically proven (Q.E.D.). Authorities always get the last word, if listeners accept the premises of the argument.

Reminder: Language is the key to understanding Value Systems. A Value System is the language structure. Be mindful of words, as they are the programming languages of our mental computer.

Work: System 4 is the primary or secondary pattern for about 35% of the workforce and is widely distributed among all levels of the hierarchy and job classifications. Considering the great capacity for details, extended concentration, the need for perfection and an unswerving belief that there is a reason for everything, System 4's require mentally difficult tasks to be happy. Long cycle time projects, which are self-paced, rather than group or machine paced, are more challenging. The opportunity to solve problems, and highly complex puzzles is highly motivating. We have in most modern, technology-based organizations many opportunities for this value system to succeed and to contribute. That is, assuming management has "constancy of purpose" and makes changes incrementally.

Summary of System 4 – Conventional Values:

Sacrifice for a higher principle, followed by salvation for the act, gives comfort. With a highly structured set of moral rights and wrongs, the path of life is clear and straight. Rules, tradition and "shoulds" give guidance in avoiding "the road less traveled." Work is a duty. Loyalty to others of like belief is given without question. This conformity of thought leads, however, to a struggle for peace of mind. Life is faithfulness.

System 5 – Competitive

Source: Manipulative values arise when the Conventional system of thinking begins to be boring. Tentative excursions outside the comfort zone did not result in condemnation, as expected, but instead, gave intense pleasure immediately. Delaying pleasure in the here and now, while others are seen living for the here and now, creates dissonance that logical thinking cannot rationalize. The shift can also begin when the defenses of the comfort zone are destroyed and harsh reality becomes undeniable. Extreme conformity is often inhumane. Life now becomes not duty, but a competitive game.

System 5 returns the person to internal motivation, as with System 3 Cynicism, but without the crudity and brutish behavior of that earlier stage of human development. With competitiveness, cunning, calculation and cash, System 5 is learned from imitation of highly visible role models in the culture, community or corporation. Highly evolved organizations take the form of a multi-leveled pyramid with upward mobility primarily determined by socioeconomic Darwinism. Meritocracy, the model upon which market economies allegedly operate, thrives on competition and acquisition. Persons with competitive values (if competent) climb the slope of the pyramid while looking upward to emulate those nearer the peak and downward to see who may be challenging for position.

System 5 thinkers prefer to associate with others of like beliefs. Birds of this feather desire to flock together at lavish rituals with the rich and famous, notable and notorious, and the powerful and elite, in order to see and be seen. Lavish rituals are the training grounds for those who aspire to be successful and serve as conspicuous displays of success for the experienced pyramid climbers. No longer is there a need for physical force as required

47

by System 3, but sophisticated psychological force. "Friendly persuasion." The strategy is to associate with those who are winning and avoid those who are losing. The primary tactic is obsequious compliance. In the Competitive world people are separated into the "we's, they's and want-to-be's."

Needs: With a focus on carefully defined and highly desirable goals, the motivation is to take only moderate risks. A goal set too high invites failure, and a goal too low is insufficiently satisfying when attained. Nothing will be left to chance since goal setting is a calculated venture supported by well-thought-through strategies in pursuit of the objective. Physical and mental energy is needed to behave successfully, which leads to a need to be immersed in a hyperactive environment. "Lights, action, camera." A milieu of other people who are hyperactive verbally and physically is needed to maintain the high energy necessary to persist in the pursuit of goals. For this reason, Competitive people tend to attract followers with the same system of thinking as well as challengers to their leadership position. Consistent with this need for constant excitement is a preference for high noise levels, strong colors, rapidly changing audiovisual stimuli and more opportunities to talk than to listen. The need to be orally expressive is fulfilled by an audience of admirers and sycophants (self-seeking flatterers).

In addition, there is one more strong need —financial opportunity. In the capitalist system, success is measured by money. Objectives will not be pursued unless they can be measured. The goal must have a monetary value or it is truly "not worth it." In the Competitive game of life, money is the way one keeps score.

Wants: The consequence of successful competition is winning the trophy; a powerful motivator for System 5 thinking, for it also gives automatic widespread and highly visible recognition of achievement. The trophies may be inanimate statues or a high profile public presence (attractive, rich, famous, well-married, etc.), triggering jealousy in others, it is hoped. Things are wanted which are highly prized (houses, vehicles, jewelry, money, "significant others" etc.) and evoke envy from the admirers and public. The motive is to have it all and then more, which leads to focused drive and possibly "success." With this desire to be the superstar is a suspicion of the motives of the competition and wariness of surprise attacks. Competitive people often express these ideas in sports or warfare terms.

Life and Death: Death is courted, teased and provoked through pursuing high levels of activity and physical stress taken to the maximum limits (the "no pain, no gain" credo). Death is another competitor to beat in the game of life. Out-maneuvering and outsmarting death is another measure of success. One strategy to assure a lasting victory is to immortalize one's conquests. Leaving a tangible legacy in the form of a monument, work of art, science or commerce, foundation or family is the ultimate conquest of death in an immortal form. And when facing death, the risk taking and gambling aspect of life extends to relationships with God in the form of bribes ("give me another chance, and I'll make it worth your while by becoming a more deserving person"). The motive and motto is "live fast and die young" and make the departure swift and highly visible. No slowly fading away of life into the sunset of death.

Time and Space: The past, to System 5 thinkers, is quite short, for the past is of relatively little concern for the simple reason that it is "past." What is done is done and cannot be altered, although it is subject to reinterpretation to suit one's current posturing. The future is, on the other hand, subject to influence, malleable, and amenable to manipulation. No longer does the past determine the future, as with System 4, but can be anything one wants it to be, given sufficient planning and dedicated energy. We have, therefore, a forward looking value system in which, given the resources, most anything can be accomplished and even the sky is no longer the limit. With the formulation of a distant goal, the intermediate time from now to then can be carefully and strategically planned. This expansionist thinking of time correlates with the continuous

49

expansion of space. Faster, bigger, better, merge, acquire, push the limits, expand the envelope and enlarge — growth is good. Whatever is beyond the current limits will be the next territory to be conquered.

Love and Hate: An acquisitive value system loves the things money can buy. This is not limited to inanimate objects, but can include humans ("trophy wives and husbands"), albeit ones who are treated as possessions. Things are public displays of success (as defined by System 5 values), in particular, things that carry a highly visible logo/brand name considered prestigious.

Opposite to the love of things is hate (fear) of the "lower classes," in the sense of being farther down the socioeconomic pyramid. The "they's" are considered not to be less fortunate, but less motivated. However, competitive people do accept the existence of "them" for they form the lower level and wide supporting base of the pyramid. The disdain for the lower classes also stems from the belief that "they" do not contribute to the welfare of the nation, but only take "welfare" from those who have achieved or are pursuing financial success.

Competitive values encourage a love of fads and fashion. To look out for number one and be the front runner in the race for the gold medals of life it is necessary to be at the forefront of lifestyle and compete with others in a manipulative game of "status-enhancement." Food, automotive and clothing fads compete with fads in investment, management and marketing. However, when the fads become part of the mainstream popular culture, they are abandoned as out-of-date and replaced with the latest fashion, whether or not it is any more appropriate.

When it comes to the relationships between competitive men and women, love takes the form of a manipulative *quid pro quo* transaction of "giving in order to get." The other sex, in other words, is used. However, to get the best possible deal requires careful negotiation and proper presentation and packaging of what one offers in exchange. In part, it is love for another person and, in part, the love of making a successful deal.

Content and Process: With the high energy levels often associated with Competitive values comes the ability to process big chunks of data. There is no reason to go slowly in communicating data to System 5 thinkers. The need to quantify and measure goals and progress in pursuit of those goals leads to the acquirement of computational skills. The focus on results, more than the means of attaining goals, permits the content of nonsequential data to be understood as long as it is clearly connected to distant goals. If not connected to personal goals, the information will not be received well, nor will it be well received.

Feedback that does not correlate with the positive attainment of goals is rejected. In other words, only positive feedback is accepted, and negative data is filtered. The net result of this pattern is actually zero feedback, since only the positive is accepted and the negative is rejected, the influence on behavior is essentially zero. As discussed in the earlier section on comfort zones, only negative feedback permits change, providing it is not excessive. The rejection of negative feedback keeps System 5 Competitive persons in a positive thinking and upbeat mode. The attention span may be long or quite short. That is conditional upon whether the information or other person presents a strategic advantage in the achievement of objectives.

Language: Competitive values place an emphasis on assuring that one's vocabulary is contemporary. Vogue "catch" phrases and faddish words are incorporated into the spoken terminology early in their invention as a way of demonstrating to others that one is up-to-date and on the leading edge. That is, until they are out of vogue because they have entered the mainstream, whereupon they are dropped in favor of what is now the newest voguish vocabulary. A positive mental attitude is communicated to others in a style that is persuasive, extroverted, energetic and seductive. Competitiveness gives people significant opportunities for leadership of people with this same value system. To persons who do not share the same language style, however, the tone is likely to be perceived as condescending with an air of superiority.

Competitiveness being the basic motivator, every transaction is a win-lose debate that continues until one person quits or loses in the verbal jousting. The winner of the contest gets the last word and the right to make the decision. Words are the psychological means of influencing behavior in others and money is the validation that the behavior is correct.

Work: System 5 is the primary or secondary pattern for about 15% of the total workforce and more often found in exempt, managerial and marketing job classifications. The need for action creates a requirement that work be variable in content, such as is characteristic of professions, management and sales. While the focus is on the future, the cycle time from start to finish of a project needs to be of medium length, in the range of months, not days or decades. The individuality and competitiveness precludes true teamwork, and machine or group-paced activities are shunned in favor of self-paced ones. The goal-focused thinking also requires that an individualized reward is possible. Training is best done individually and informally to accommodate the individualistic style and ego.

Summary of System 5 – Competitive: The need for leadership opportunities creates an entrepreneurial orientation to life and work. Success is measured in materialism and money. The need to achieve and be successful drives the thinking, and consequently, behavior. Motivation is spurred by objectives with strategies to pursue the goals. Science and rational thought provide the means to contrive tactics to make the strategies efficient. In summary, life is a game and "the one with the most toys wins."

System 6 — Compassionate

Source: Sociocentric thinking is a sharp divergence from the prior system. When high achievers cannot escape feedback that they are strongly disliked for their selfishness (or have manipulative parents) it destroys their comfort zone. They begin to develop sensitivity to the feelings of others. When material goods no longer satisfy the need for identity, vague feelings of a spiritual void come forth. Subjectivity replaces objectivity in a search for new meanings in life. Subjective ideas, having no proof or disproof of their validity, are accepted as true. Anti-scientific thinking permits the whole-hearted acceptance of "non-disprovable" hypotheses and ideas ("if it cannot be disproved, then it must be true").

The peer group is a significant source of Compassionate values. In the search for meaning of life through the lives of others, companions all have equal rights and equally valid views. Diversity is not just tolerated, but relished, and the awareness of differences among ethnic cultures is celebrated. All views are equally true, even though different. Facts are subordinate to feelings. Feelings become the primary reality and must be shared to make them ever more real. All of these sources for the development of System 6 thinking operate in an open, nonjudgmental environment overflowing with creative activities.

Among the many and varied sources of such an open and loosely structured value system are: New Age, Eastern-derived and unity-focused religions and the belief in psychic phenomena and paranormal psychology.

Needs: As the nonjudgmental perspective broadens its horizons, a need for total acceptance strengthens. Being accepted as one is, not for what one does, expands the comfort zone. Tolerance from others is expected; the limits of tolerance need to be tested. Forgiveness is presumed to be unlimited in scope and unerring in separating an evil act from the human actor. Compassionate caring is not just expected; it is a strongly and deeply felt need.

Closure is to be avoided. Finishing something brings closure, and with closure comes the end of creativity and consequently judgment. One's life is considered to be a "work in progress", as are life's activities. There is no need to be concerned with "closing of the loops" and finishing a task. The process of creating **is** the motivator, not the finished product, so there is no need to strive for completion. Creation has no beginning nor end for it is perceived as "pure process", not "content." A chaotic environment of rapid and radical change facilitates creative activities. A seemingly stable situation can instantly disintegrate into a jumble only to reform like a kaleidoscope. Compassionate people thrive on chaos as an opportunity for creativity. Since the "universal mind" directs the turn of events, there is no need for worry and consequently no need for a backup system.

Wants: System 6 requires no proof of worthiness, no display of acquisitions, no accolades for achievement. Self-worth no longer comes from net worth. There is no reason to prove one's existence or validate by deeds. One can **be** by doing nothing. To be totally accepting of life's situation, to be forgiving of transgressions, to be a faithful friend, to be an equal — these are the core values and are, therefore, the antithesis of Competitive values. (There is a conflict between Systems 5 and 6 on major issues: capitalism versus socialism, individuals versus group, personal responsibility versus shared culpability, and the distribution of income and opportunities.)

Life and Death: The permeable boundary between self and other humans expands to include all life forms and the preservation of all species — particularly animal — and protection from the miasma of corrupt institutions. The biosphere, mother earth, the green planet and other environmental concerns exceed the concern for one's own death, which is unimportant in the larger perspective. The openness of this thinking process permits Compassionate people to treat death as an illusion. If the universe is really about process and not tangible content, then the earth is truly a living organism. All things flow together in a swirling mixture of life. Humans have no special position. This is the value system from which humanist concerns for the dignity and welfare of people emanate.

Time and Space: In a world of process, having no special beginning or end, time becomes irrelevant. The future is a short (very short) time away and the past is nearby. The idea derives from the concept that only humans "time-bind". No other life form segregates events into time frames; therefore, time is neither real nor particularly important.

If death is illusionary, being an artificial construct of Conventional values, so may time and space be illusions. In a universe of process, only **mind** exists. Time, therefore, is an artificial invention of humans having no real existence. Space is also an illusion, and its dimensions are another human contrivance. "Time-space coordinates" operate in a synchronicity of all sentient beings. Time and space are relegated to the category of erroneous attempts to control and master a universe which humans perversely perceive as possessing.

Love and Hate: Compassion is for people, not things. Loving people, especially people who are in desperate need of love, evokes empathy and sympathy. Feeling the pain of others and responding to it satisfies a deep need of System 6 for humanism. Conversely, "things" are not worthy of love and may even be hated for being a barrier to closeness with people. When objects are more loved than are people, Compassionate persons are derisive of those who possess those objects. In this system of thinking, love is a two-way process and objects cannot give love, nor, therefore, should they receive any affection. Objects are to be used; people are to be loved. (This is the opposite of System 5 thinking.)

55

Compassionate values exude love to all those who need it, particularly the helpless, loveless and victims of abuse and persecution. People who need people, need people who need help. If someone is "help-less," it presents an opportunity to share time, money, possessions and feelings — as much as it takes, as long as it takes, as many times as it takes. Judgement and condemnation of others for their transgressions is withheld, unless those errors are seen as deliberately intended to hurt people, then severe judgment will follow. Individuals or institutions that abuse people or the environment are targets for revenge — at the least, passive civil disobedience, at the most, deadly destruction.

Another form of love for people is seeking consensus, in the strict sense of total and complete agreement among all participants. It is another way of assuring that no feelings will be hurt. Leadership and group decision-making is neither conventional nor manipulative charismatic leadership, but rather facilitation of the group process. The content or quality of the decision is less important than the process of reaching full, unrestrained consensus without inflicting any discomfort upon anyone's feelings. The power is with the people who form the team and share the same vision and values. (A popular System 6 theme exploited by System 5)

Relationships, a System 6 term for interaction between (or among) the sexes, is a physical and/or mental union of shared beliefs and pleasures. These may be brief encounters or sustained commitments and not necessarily within the conventional and traditional male-female definition of a relationship.

Content and Process: Needing to deal with the process of learning as much or more than the content of the subject matter, Compassionate learners (and instructors) thoroughly explore small chunks of information a piece at a time. The learning process proceeds in a nonsequential fashion. The absorption of the data and ideas is not rote drill but alignment of ideas within an

56

ideological framework. All topics are sociopolitical in a Sociocentric value system.

The need to be nonjudgmental leads to the rejection of feedback — whether given or received. Grading, rating, classifying and calibrating are forms of judging the value of another (especially children and the "disadvantaged") and are to be avoided (a major source of conflict with Conventional values). In such an open and creative thought process there is no need to focus on goals or ends, but rather, to remain unfocused and let the process develop in a "natural" way. This is accompanied with a very long attention span (time is not a relevant dimension).

Language: The subjectivity of System 6 is expressed in a language style which revolves around a non-specific, subjective vocabulary. Objective, visible, tangible referents are avoided for that would restrict ideas/feelings from flowing freely in meandering, incomplete phrases. Concomitant with this openness of language is the origin of "Politically Correct" (PC) wherein ethnocentric, gender, physical, socioeconomic or racial terms are scorned, particularly those originating with Western male-oriented cultures. (Which has led to curious combinations and circumlocutions to avoid "discrimination").

The most extreme extension of this approach (or avoidance) to conventional language is the "deconstruction" movement. In this phenomenon, the meaning is not imbedded within the text by the author, but rather it is subject to interpretation to fit the group ideology. Words are signs that refer to other words, which refer to yet other words and are not to be trusted, so redefinition of conventional words to fit the group's (and cult's) idiosyncratic beliefs. This language style also serves to obfuscate meaning.

Speaking styles vary from passive to aggressive, depending on whether the intended listener is perceived as friend or foe. The peer group and the disadvantaged and put-upon of society receive passive acceptance and soft tones; the enemy (institutions and the rich and powerful) receives a vociferous and harsh attack.

The focus on the group process in the desire for consensus means closure is to be avoided, or at least delayed until everyone has had an opportunity to participate. Sociocentric meetings tend to run on, so everyone gets another word into the transaction.

Work: System 6 is the primary or secondary pattern for about 10% of the total workforce and widely distributed among all job classes. Appealing activities are ones which help humankind, nurture the needy, aid the ill, defend the downtrodden, avenge the abused, counsel the confused and bring about a more egalitarian world. However, so do creative activities in the graphic arts, music, dance, performance and helping children and adults develop their full human potential.

The Compassionate person works best when there is no cycle time, that is, any rigidly imposed limits that would interfere with the helping process. Group activities, in which the pacing is up to the group to determine, combined with an open environment, are preferred, thus giving opportunities for interactive learning from other members of the team.

Summary of System 6 - Compassionate: Essential to the expression of this value system is people and the chance to belong to something worthwhile in the larger world perspective. Harmony among peers and friendship with many others who need befriending, fills needs for meaningful relationships. Anti-materialism rejects the world's abundance of greed that is harmful to humankind. Affiliation with others of like beliefs is the prime motivator. Subjectivity is favored over objectivity. Sensitivity is offered to those who suffer from the unfeeling of others. Life is equality.

System 7 – Conscious

Source: Existential thinking emphasizes the individual's unique position as a self-determining agent, responsible for the authenticity of his or her choices and the consequences of one's behavior. No easy excuses, no false blaming, no victim poses. As the values shift progresses, the fear of disapproval by valued others becomes irrelevant and the outer edge of the comfort zone dissolves. Judgement of behavior or beliefs moves away from absolutism to relativism. The question is no longer whether something right or wrong, but rather, is it appropriate to the current situation?

If one goes outside the comfort zone, there are available a wide range of new and different ideas. Conscious values can develop. There are multiple channels for Conscious values: internal rethinking of currently held views, input from new external sources (people, books, film, theater and travel) — personal experience being the most powerful. Sources are not judged as right or wrong but rather as effective versus ineffective, appropriate versus inappropriate.

Needs: As the need for a binary (is, is not) world decreases, the need for a world with a flexible structure increases. "Yes and No" answers are amended with "Maybe." Standard responses become variable; tasks are completed only if it is appropriate to close the loop while others are put "on hold," and the answer to many of life's questions is "it depends."

Rewards and punishments are not needed by System 7, and consequently have diminished effect on behavior. Interpersonal transactions in which another person or the institution dangles carrots and brandishes sticks are no longer effective motivators.

Reward, if received, will be accepted. Punishment, if given, will be accepted. In neither case, however, was the event a cause of the antecedent behavior, but simply a natural consequence. **In nature, there are no rewards or punishments — just consequences.**

The strong need for new experiences in this experientially driven value system does lead to positive and negative consequences, but it does not cause nor deter the experimentation (much to the chagrin of those using conformist or manipulative techniques.) System 7's response to error is, "So, what did we learn?"

Wants: Conscious people learn who they are by what they do. Societal and industrial classifications, titles, certificates and demographic labels (age, race, sex, and the plethora of "hyphenated Americans") do not carry as much meaning as they do for all the other value systems. It is the difference between being a "verb" or being a "noun", a "thing" or an "action." New ideas and new people are "conditionally accepted" with a mild positive attitude, but still conditional on the appropriateness or inappropriateness to the current situation. Again, "it depends."

A powerful motivator for System 7 is being a teacher of others, a student of others and a colleague to all who have something to contribute to knowledge. Whether in positions of leadership or "follower-ship", opportunities for teaching, learning and exchanging ideas are strongly desired. Any experience, whether positive or negative, which results in learning is considered a good experience. There is no need for reward or punishment.

Life and Death: System 7 accepts that there is a beginning to life and an end at death, but without delineating precisely when each event occurs. It is what happens. Contrary to all the other value systems, there is no mind versus body duality. Mind is **not** a noun, but a **verb** (the way the brain/computer works). The idea of a "mind" living somehow beyond death of the brain is not accepted on faith, but simply a hypothesis that has not been personally tested. Heaven and hell are irrelevant variations of the "no rewards or punishments in nature" theme. The motto is "live moderate and die moderate," with nothing to excess and to prolong life, not just because it is sacred, but to have time for new experiences. Further, if life is not sacred, then death is not tragic (it is what happens). God is a **verb.**

Time and Space: The past is there to learn from, so as not to perpetuate inappropriate responses to new situations. The present is the "not past." With these existential dichotomies System 7 engages in **"what ifs."** "What if that past event were present now? What could we learn that is appropriate or inappropriate to the current situation?" "What if the future were now? What would we be doing?" In other words, the past verb tense is treated **as if** it were present tense, and the future tense is treated **as if** it were now. The purpose is to bring events from other times, past or future, into the present, for it is only in the present that action occurs. Time is an active process of what is happening as it actually happens. Time is a dependent variable.

Space is another dependent variable. How far, how close, how big, how small, how soon? It depends on the tactics, which in turn depend on the strategies, which depend on the objectives. Conscious thinking is highly logical, but quite situational. The thought process begins with carefully constructed objectives. Once the objectives crystallize they are likely to remain constant for a long time. Strategies support objectives and must provide a clear schema for arranging available resources in pursuit of the objectives. Strategies, if well conceived, last several years, minimum. Finally, tactics make the strategy work effectively, but may be dramatically modified or abandoned whenever they prove ineffective or inappropriate. By this hierarchical thought process, conscious awareness thrives.

Love and Hate: Situations that might be changed or improved are appealing to System 7. If it cannot be changed, even for the sake of change, then the thrill is gone and hate for the *status quo* results in a quick exit in search of an opportunity to experiment. There is a love for discomforting experiences, ideas and events

61

that take one out of the comfort zone. For to System 7, these are the means to learning. Since the limits of the comfort zone have dissolved, or become permeable, each discomforting experience leads to the need for another. Being programmed by institutions, authorities and the socially powerful is hated for it is seen as an attempt to impose a constricted comfort zone.

Love is mutual acceptance. Quirks and peccadilloes are accepted — not positively appreciated — just accepted.

Content and Process: Conscious learning accepts information in any size bite and any sequence. The thinking is non-linear, so the acquisition of knowledge is not necessarily linear.

Pattern recognition is one of the strong features of System 7 thoughts. Conscious people search for and want to find a pattern. If it is appropriate to the situation and effective, then it becomes an algorithm (a predictable process and set of rules for solving problems.) Algorithms require no new thinking because they work every time, if correctly designed. Certain quotidian chores may become algorithms therefore requiring little time or energy from the person, thus releasing these resources to create heuristics. Heuristics are the converse of algorithms. Heuristics include hunches, "what ifs" and yet-to-be-tested hypotheses. When the hypothesis proves wrong, it is dropped and another is tried, and perhaps another, until it is validated and proven reliable and thus it becomes an algorithm. Then the next heuristic is created. Thus achieving a balance of effective process with appropriate content.

Language: Words are used by System 7 in a search for precise and concise terminology with which to think. Accuracy in vocabulary is highly valued since the brain/computer is a word processor and needs exactness to process information effectively and efficiently. English, for example, with an extensive vocabulary, (combinations of old German and French, with heavy additions from many other languages) has more than sufficient words with which to be precise. System 7 revels in language. Phrases are simple, concise and to the point. If phrases are complex — "decomplex".

Speaking tone varies according to the situation; whatever is appropriate. Closure occurs if it is possible to make an effective and appropriate decision. Otherwise, delay. The major decision-maker is he or she who has to follow through. With the opportunity to make a decision, it is appropriate that one accepts personal responsibility for the consequences.

Work: System 7 is the primary or secondary pattern for about 10% of the all employees and concentrated in exempt job classifications. It should be evident by now that System 7 requires activities with variable content and variable processes. The time-cycle may be short or long, but there must be variety. This implies self-paced, individual contributor or leadership roles more than being a team player. The overarching requirement is a chance to make change and learn by direct experience from the work itself.

Summary of System 7 – Conscious Values: Key attributes are spontaneity and flexibility in thought and action. The need for personal growth through direct personal experiences is pervasive. With a goal-orientation and need for actualization of potential comes a restlessness for **doing as the path to being**. Problems are framed as creative learning opportunities. System 7 has moved beyond survival to being. Life is all about acceptance and change.

We have described pure values. All of us are mixtures in various aspects of our thinking.

With these descriptions of the various system of thinking comes the opportunity to understand the reason for behavior, not just the behavior itself. Value systems go beyond what someone is doing into the realm of **why.**

Employee Feedback from CVR Attitude Surveys

From 24 years of interviews, meeting with 1000's of employees to discuss the results of the CVR Employee Attitude Survey, employees at all levels of the hierarchy have had opportunities to express their views and values. In these group and private settings, people were asked when they had felt negative about being an employee and why. The next question asked was when had they felt positive about being an employee and why. Careful listening to the responses of the "why" question permits one to determine the primary values of the person or group. Here are representative responses selected from the most recent five years of their candid comments, categorized by the eight dimensions identified within section one entitled The We/They Gap.

System 2 Values – Clannish

Trust Among Levels of Hierarchy

Negative Comments:

"The bad thing about working here on the line is all these new college kids coming in as supervisors, they call them 'team leaders, and these people do not know how to do the jobs that we do, in fact they do not bother to learn. What is the point of having supervisors if they can't help you do the job better."

"The plant manager job is always filled with someone new. At the meetings they just talk about mission and vision statements but I've never seen anyone act that way. "

(Translated from Polynesian) "We used to sing while we worked. It's a part of our tradition. It helps us get through the shift without becoming bored. Singing makes us happy. When we got a new plant manager from the states a couple of years ago, he put a stop to it. Said it interfered with productivity."

"If the HR guy tells me one more time that he wants to 'make a deposit in my emotional bank account' I'm going to tell my husband and he'll come down here and beat him up!"

"Ever since we got self-directed here at the plant you can't ask a supervisor anything since we are supposed to make all our own decisions. I don't like that since it means the supervisor can't tell us what to do anymore."

"Why does management keep pushing this empowerment thing at us? They never said a word about having to do that in my job interview."

Positive Comments:

"You know, we've had the same managers a long time and they treat us just like family. None of that air of high and mighty. It's kind of like everybody trusts each other. When those corporate types are coming to visit our managers and supervisors let us know so that we can look sharp and be on our best behavior. We call the tour the parade route."

"Ever since management gave up on that team stuff and gave us a real supervisor instead of a "facilitator", things are getting better. I still don't understand what is wrong with having someone you can find when you need him and ask questions about what the hell we should do when something doesn't go right."

(Translated from Spanish) "The best thing about working here? Having a supervisor ('jefe' = chief/boss) who knows some

Spanish. He doesn't speak it very good, but he tries. It is really a lot of fun, because I'm learning more English."

"Finally they paved our parking lot. It used to be mud and when it rained your car could slide down the hill. You didn't see any of the managers parking their cars in the mud. They parked in the visitor spots. They still do, but that is okay because they've got our parking lot covered in asphalt now."

"Last month when we hit out numbers, our night shift supervisor cooked steaks for everyone right out here on the loading dock. He wore an apron and one of those tall hats the cooks wear on TV. We had a lot of fun kidding him about it."

"Whenever we have a perfect safety month, the coffee vending machines are free. Not a big deal but it shows the man in the corner office knows we are out here."

Freedom from Retribution

Negative Comments:

"You know, around here they tell us to speak our mind. But if you say anything that they don't like, they say you have a bad attitude and hand you a business card of some shrink to get your attitude adjusted. It doesn't pay to believe all the 'mission' stuff that they hang on the walls about all those fancy statements of beliefs."

"Why do we get punished for using a benefit? They tell us we get sick days but they go against your attendance record. Why don't they just give us the sick days and then start counting after that?"

"You know, they started a job enrichment program around here about a year ago. This consultant started the program. She said it would make everyone happy. It's done nothing but create confusion and frustration and when you do new stuff you get in trouble for it."

"At the end of the month, everything goes out the window to make shipping numbers. We ship product knowing it is bad and will be returned but our supervisor doesn't care."

"Open Door Policy! The doors are always shut in your face."

"The Open Door here leads to the unemployment line."

Positive Comments:

"One thing I like about management here, I can go straight to the top, cause we have an open door policy and it really works. Sometimes you don't get the answer you wanted but at least you get an answer. As a matter of fact, the supervisors will make it a point to make sure you get to see the top guy and will even make the appointment for you. And the best thing is that you don't have to worry about what you say."

(Translated from Vietnamese) "Here at the wiring plant all 700 workers are Vietnamese. All our supervisors are Vietnamese. There is a lady in human resources who is Vietnamese and we can go to her anytime we want to for help on insurance. One of the top men is married to a Vietnamese. It's like one big family. We all understand everyone's thinking. And we won an award from IBM and the award in on the wall."

"You know, you can count on management following through with what they say. You don't have to worry about any double standards. Everyone follows the same rules, regardless of who your supervisor is and we all get treated the same."

"We have had some change in the top bosses. And I've worked here for thirty years. The nice thing is that none of these new bosses try and change the things that have become tradition around here like the summer picnic."

67

Communication and Feedback about Performance

Negative Comments:

"You know that old saying, 'no news is good news', well that sure is true around here cause the only news you get is bad. Regardless of how much we do or how much we ship, the front office is never satisfied. If you hit the goal, they make the playing field longer. Managers like to talk about business like it is a football game but they always change the rules of the game."

(Translated from Spanish) "Lots of people here speak Spanish. Do you think the human resource manager can speak Spanish? No way! They don't even put out the stuff on the bulletin board in Spanish. Something about the state law says they don't have to."

"Management tells us that we are a big team and we are all in this together. They have a program about providing us information on our job performance. But the feedback doesn't come but once a year. Why can't they tell us immediately when we are doing something wrong?"

"Every time there is a problem, some head honcho in the office puts out a memo about the problem. We never hear it from our supervisor. What's wrong with the supervisor showing us the problem and telling us how to fix it?"

Positive Comments:

"Ever since they started putting up these charts, I mean BIG charts, about how we're doing you don't have to wait for the supervisor to tell you how you are doing. You sure don't have to wait for those quarterly big get-togethers on how you're doing. If you want to know – just look at the chart."

"Whenever my supervisor sees me doing something that is not right, she tells me about it and then shows me how to correct it.

It's nice to have a boss that understands your job and lets you know how you are doing and shows you how to do better."

"You can understand management talk around here. They do not use those fifty-dollar words from the puzzle palace (H.Q.). When they explain something, they explain it in a way that you can use. And you can explain it to your family."

"My supervisor tries to have daily meetings with us as a work group. If she can't, she takes the time to talk to everyone in the department and tell us what is going on."

Cooperation Among and Within Work Groups and Teams

Negative Comments:

"All this self-directed stuff doesn't make any sense. Why don't they just tell us what they want and we'll take care of it. Ever since we stopped having supervisors and got team leaders this place has gone down hill. Also they put these charts on the wall to show how each shift did. Now we have to compete with the other shifts and we don't have time to clean up."

"Why does management have our group results posted on the bulletin board for everyone to see. They talk a big game about teamwork and cooperation then make us compete with every other work group."

"Our supervisor won't let us cooperate with the other work groups. She is just too busy trying to make herself look good. The supervisors don't cooperate with one another. They are just in here to make a name for themselves."

"Why don't other shifts have to clean up like us?"

"Every time that I offer to help people in another department, my supervisor tells me it's their problem, not ours. So I should stay out of it. I used to work there and could help them but I'm not allowed to."

Positive Comments:

"We don't have any problem getting along with each other. We have all been here a long time. Every once in a while someone might have a bad day because of something at home, but we accept that. That's the way life is."

"Our supervisor helps us work out problems that occur on the line. I mean, if another department is creating a problem for our work group, he will talk with the other group to get cooperation."

"We all get along within our group. And the supervisor knows it. She encourages us to cooperate with one another and with the people in other work groups."

"Our shift comes in 15 minutes before the other one leaves. We're supposed to find out what's going on and it helps us get along with them."

"When ever there is a management meeting, the managers come out and tell us which areas need help and then let us volunteer to help them out. They promote cooperation."

Freedom from Favoritism and Discrimination

Negative Comments:

"I don't see why we should have to work with people who are not like us. I mean, these people coming in seem to be able to get away with anything. Nobody says a word to them. If those people are going to work here, then I think they should be able to do the job, keep their mouth shut and get along – or get out. But management just puts up with it."

"Our temps aren't disciplined like we are when they are absent or late. If I am absent or late, I catch hell, but the temp working next to me – nobody says anything to her. When I complained to the supervisor, she told me to mind my own business. I just think that they know if they make the temps mad, they will quit."

"The bidding process is a joke. Our supervisor tells us what the rules are and then selects whomever he decides he wants. If you just smile and flirt a little then you can get picked."

"You get promoted if you play golf, otherwise forget it."

"Management says that they are encouraging diversity. But how many people in management are like us. There are no women and there are no Asians. Tell me that there is no favoritism!"

Positive Comments:

"Our supervisor expects everyone to do the job and he doesn't care who you are, where you came from or who your mama and daddy were. He is fair with everybody even if he is kind of tough sometimes. At least he's tough on everyone the same."

"Our boss is really a tough person. But everyone knows exactly where they stand with him. At least he treats everyone the same."

"Our management group believes what they say. There are both younger and older people in top management. They don't favor the young ones like many companies do."

"Our management made sure that all groups are represented in upper management. That way we know that all groups have fair representation."

Having a Positive Outlook for the Future

Negative Comment:

"You know, the human resource manager, she asked me once, what I was going to do with my life. I just told her, this **is** my life! I just hope I last long enough to make it to retirement."

"It's not like it used to be here anymore since we got bought out by that Korean company. Those people can't treat us like they do their own people. It is hotter than hell in the melt shop and we don't get but 25 cents an hour more. But who is gonna stop them except the UAW. Just wait until the election.

It's no fun. You can't talk, the breaks are 15 minutes but it takes 5 minutes to walk each way to the ladies' room. So I just put in my eight hours and go home."

"I was on a shift that worked well for my family. You know both my husband and I work. Then management changed everything. Now I can't get to my shift because they want temporary people on my shift. How can I have a good future when temporaries are doing my work on the shift I need to help my family?"

"I was told that we all got time off during the summer months because business was slow at that time. That was great because my kids were out of school and I could spend time with them. Now management has developed this 'core' and 'seasonal' work force idea. Now none of us can get the schedule we want for our families because the core people have to work one schedule and the seasonal people get to elect to work. And if you become seasonal, you don't get the benefits."

"The work here is not steady. They use people's jobs as a cost cutting measure. You can count on the fact that if the numbers aren't good, many of us will be laid off for a short period of time and everyone else ends up working overtime."

Positive Comment:

"I don't expect to ever get promoted, but that's ok. If they make you a supervisor you get more work and you don't get any overtime pay. So long as I can do better for my family and their future, that's all I ask for."

"My supervisor is really good. She understands when you have personal problems that need to get fixed. She gives us the time and knows that we work better when we come back. We would all do anything we could for her."

"This company has been really good. They try to let us go to the shifts we need to meet our family schedules. The benefits are good. They take care of you. The pay is steady. You can count on it."

"If you make a mistake the supervisor helps you correct the problem and teaches you how to do it right. That is good. If we are all doing things right that means better job security."

(Translated from Polynesian) "The new big-boss told us he wanted us to sing like we used to. You should have seen the look on everyone's face. Like a sunrise over the horizon. It is good to have a big-boss who understands our ways."

Opportunities to Use Skills and Abilities

Negative Comments:

"Management keeps telling us to be creative, whatever that means. Every time I try something or do more things and try to show them that I know how to do it, I'm told I'm getting out of line. I'm told to go just do my job."

"We've all done this job for a lot of years. Management now thinks we have to prove ourselves by taking a test. What good is

73

that? When we can do the job right what is a test going to prove?"

"When someone in my group has the ability to do something new, my supervisor tells them that they aren't qualified because they don't have the schooling. I mean, if that person can do the job, then why does management stop them because of a piece of paper?"

"Management tells us to approach the problem like we have never seen it before. They call it 'thinking out of the box.' Then I hear them laughing at some of the ideas. Why would anyone want to stick their neck out to use their skills when management is going to laugh?"

Positive Comments:

"I like the way we get to do new stuff and different things. It kind of keeps you sharp. And these training programs we have here are kind of fun. It keeps your brain alive. It also helps me keep up with my kids."

"They seem concerned that we are keeping up with the times, whatever that is supposed to mean. But they offer us training at good times and the classes are short. We get the information one step at a time and a chance to practice."

"Management listens to us when we talk about the things that we can do. They let us try it. They do not listen to those consultants first. They make the consultants listen to us first. Then we slowly start to make the changes. It's slow. There is a lot of training. But we really feel good about it."

"Its great when my boss allows me to try things that I learned at my prior company. They taught me a lot and my supervisor knows that. So she doesn't mind when I try something different. Not everything I know was learned here at this job."

Fair and Equitable Compensation

Negative Comments:

"I get darn tired of all the big guys getting all the money. They get big cars, big houses and big bonuses. They keep telling us about all the profits the company keeps making – and why not – it's coming out of our pockets. Now they are going to start something called pay for performance. How's that going to work when they are also preaching teamwork? Won't that just start us fighting with each other? Why don't they stick to the cost of living so that we don't get behind?"

"Management keeps trying to tell us that you have to look at your 'total compensation' and how much the company paid for health insurance for us. Why do they expect us to buy that garbage? Benefits are benefits and pay is pay. They owe us the benefits and it is not part of a 'hidden paycheck', like H.R. calls it"

"Here they pay us minimum wage plus 75 cents. After a year you get one cent extra for seniority. The next year another penny and after 10 years a dime. The only time we get a raise here is when the minimum wage goes up. Then we get the lecture about the competition from the other chicken processing plants and they can't afford to pay anymore. There's a dozen new company Cadillac's for the 'head shed' out in the visitor's parking lot. Go check for yourself."

"What is this pay 'at risk' that they keep talking about? I've got a family to feed. Maybe if I made their kind of money then I could afford to have some money 'at risk'. But not on what I get. I need a paycheck that I can count on."

"If there really are pay surveys why don't we get to see them?"

Positive Comments:

"We all get paid the same after you've been around for awhile. I mean, seniority counts for something here. Every year we get a cost of living raise and all of us out here in the warehouse get the same money because we move around, we help each other, so money doesn't get in the way of doing your job."

"We can count on our paychecks around here. Management tells us what we make per hour and then we get that amount. There isn't none of this so-called 'pay for performance'. I know exactly how much I have for groceries, rent and clothes. That's all that matters."

"We all get the same money for doing the same work. No one is viewed as being better or more important. And with the system, you get extra for experience in the job after you work the job for five years. We don't get into competition with each other over pennies per hour like at my mom's company, cause we aren't in competition with each other."

"Management put in this gain sharing system. I guess its okay. The nice thing is that management doesn't get anything if we don't get anything. You can not count on it, but at least everyone is treated the same under the program."

"We can get to the top of our wage rate in just one year."

System 3 Values – Cynical

Trust Among Levels of Hierarchy

Negative Comments:

"I don't believe anything those F****** guys say. We've been lied to so many times that I just tune them out. How can I trust someone that doesn't listen? Management talks, talks, talks – but won't answer questions. All they say is 'I'll get back to you' but they never do. When this place started and I hired on, I was told that there would be promotions from within. But every one of the supervisors is from out of state. How can you trust managers who can't speak plain English? How the hell am I supposed to figure out what they're saying if they can't talk sense?"

"Management put up a chain link fence between where we park and where they park. They've got the guard in a tower in the middle. They never said if that was to protect our cars or theirs. I'll bet its just theirs."

"I got carpal tunnel syndrome from running this machine. I went to the company doctor and he sent me to the human resources department. They said I couldn't get workers comp because it's an illness and not an injury. That's the only answer that they'll give me."

"Management keeps talking to us about the competition. Anyone can see it is just their way of trying to convince us to be satisfied with low raises while they get the entire goody off the top. They took away our hot food service but look at the new company cars in the parking lot. They say it's to be competitive. I say it's to take advantage of me and the money that I make them. How do you trust someone like that?"

Positive Comments:

"This new manager we have is no-nonsense, straight out and you never have to wonder where you stand with her. If you do it right she says so. If you are doing wrong you're going to hear about that too. Loud and clear!"

"Man, I've got a great supervisor. He is the toughest person around here. He can tell when the games are going on and isn't afraid to put a stop to it. No BS with him. Nobody crosses him either. Best boss I've ever had!"

"They sent this new guy, Teddy out here to put this distribution center in order, and he sure did. He wasn't here one day before he called me into his office and slammed the door and told me what he was going to do to me if I gave him any trouble. He even talked about my mama! That's okay because we speak the same language. Turns out he came from the same old neighborhood where I grew up as a kid. Now all the rest of the guys think we're buddies and it's my job to keep them straight and stop them from stealing. Teddy's my man!"

"When the big shot VP comes out here he won't talk to me. Just goes past my forklift with his nose in the air like he smelled something bad. That doesn't bother me because as soon as he passes by I hand-signal that he is *numero uno* in my book." (Authors note: egocentrics consider such behavior to be positive.)

"We've got this human resources manager so scared that he started carrying mace in a holster in his hip like it was a 9 millimeter." (Note: System 3 considers intimidation of others as positive.)

"How can you have trust when plant mangers change ever eighteen months? Where do they go? Must have p*****-off somebody."

Freedom from Retribution

Negative Comments:

"You've got to watch everything you say to anybody. We got snitches in this group right here in this room. They are going to tell management what you say and it's going to come down on you like a ton of bricks without even a chance to explain. You speak up and you get hammered."

"Management always has its tricks. They stay awake at night looking for ways to get you on rules that have never been applied in the past."

"You don't have any freedom around here. They always make up things and change the rules just to keep me off guard. They want to fire me, but they don't have the guts to try it."

"Whenever I am working my supervisor comes over to see what I am doing. She is just trying to get something on me to try and fire me. If she keeps it up, I'll get her."

"I'm not going to say anything in this meeting because it will get back to the boss."

Positive Comments:

"If you got a gripe you can use the open door straight to the top. But, you better tell your supervisor first and give him a chance otherwise you would be in big time trouble. Now the manager just listens and never does anything, but at least I know that he got the message."

"Whenever there is a problem it is dealt with immediately. The boss may scream and throw things but everyone gets the message that he is tough and we can't put anything past him."

"Most managers we've had are wimps. They've had it easy. But my boss knows how tough life really is so he's tough, too. You need people with guts to run an organization right."

"They can do whatever they want to as long as I keep getting more money."

Communication and Feedback about Performance

Negative Comments:

 "I get tired of the boss coming out here and telling me how to do my job. He doesn't know a Phillips from a flat blade."

"Every time I bid on a job I don't get it and no one will tell me why." I just think they're afraid to say what they think. Probably afraid of the corporate lawyers.

"How can my boss think he's doing any good. He never tells me how I am doing except once a year. That doesn't count for S***."

"I am not going to trust any one to fill out forms on me on this 360 thing. I'll make sure that they understand where I am coming from and what will happen if they try pulling any tricks in this stupid process."

"How could he know what kind of work I'm doing? He's never out in the shop. Sits in his damn office playing Solitaire on his computer."

Positive Comments:

"They don't give out a lot of pats-on-the-back around here. But when you get one you know it. Now if they'd just knock off that stupid annual performance appraisal nonsense it would be even better."

"At least when you do something wrong the supervisor lets you know right then and there and what will happen if I don't change what I'm doing."

"When you are doing okay, she will tell you so and then leave you alone to do your job."

"This management is too strict on controlling everyone. But at least they do it to everyone."

Cooperation Among and Within Work Groups and Teams

Negative Comments:

"I wasn't hired to be a team player. I hired on to do my job. And all this crap about fuzzy feel good team stuff that those California-type consultants keep telling us about – you spend all your time in team meetings while this yo-yo shows you video tapes by some bald college professor."

"I was hired to do a job and now they want me to do all the jobs. This is my machine and I had to wait a long time to get it. It is the only sit down job in the place and I'm not about to give it up and rotate. And they know they can't make me because they know I'll file a discrimination charge."

"Why should I cooperate with anyone else. I know this job and don't need someone else telling me how to do it."

"Trying to cooperate with people is useless. It just slows you down and takes away the freedoms to do things like you want to do them. I'd rather work alone."

Positive Comments:

"My crew is the best damn maintenance crew in this place and we know it. And the other crews know it. Why do they waste all that money telling us we got to be a team when we've been one for years?"

"Me and the guys have known each other a long time. We know how to help each other. We don't need anyone telling how to do it. If management would just mind their own business we could get more done."

"It's a pretty good place to work once you get past all the stupid rules and regulations. It's okay to work with other people as long as they don't cut into your territory."

"It's really a tough place to work. It's dangerous. As long as people stay off our back you can get the job done right and get along."

Freedom from Favoritism and Discrimination

Negative Comments:

"There is a lot of favoritism here. Some of the people are too busy sucking up to the boss. The boss gets all her little favorites, they take all the smoke breaks they want, make excuses for being late and nothing ever happens to them. If I did that I'd get in big time trouble."

"No matter what I want to do, I'm told no. And no one ever explains why. I think they got a thing about females around here."

"They may not say it out loud, but you can tell that there is discrimination just by the way they pick on us women, especially black women, around here. I mean they claim there are rules around here and yet certain little favorites of the male managers get to do whatever they want. If this keeps up I am going to do something about it."

Positive Comments:

"There is no favoritism or discrimination around here. They kick ass on everybody."

"As long as management treats everyone poorly, then I got nothing to complain about, except the Teamsters are real interested in us."

"We may not like each other, but at least you get a straight answer and everyone gets the same answer."

"It takes a special person to work in this type of chemical operation. And management does treat everyone the same regardless of all that legal bullshit – like crap."

Having a Positive Outlook for the Future

Negative Comments:

"Why do I want to hear from management about where this company is going in the future? It never comes out that way. As far as I am concerned my future is getting the next paycheck."

"I can't get my way around here. I mean the rules are for the majority of people but not for everyone. Some of us are better than that and should be allowed to do as we please."

"Management is always changing everything. I just want my next check and with all these changes who knows if the company will be in business. We'll probably get bought by some damn foreigner."

"Management put in all these programs that you get nothing out of unless you are here for a long time. That just means they can keep the money for themselves and not treat me fairly. Who knows if you will work for any place very long."

Positive Comments:

"I figure I'll be getting another raise before too long cause I got some stuff I want to buy. Yeah, the 401(k) is good, but that's way down the road. As long as I keep healthy, I can keep working. If it don't work out here, I'll go somewhere else."

"This place is okay. They give pay raises every three months."

"I think I might stay here a little longer. I could get a raise for some of the skills I have and get more money, provided some other jerk doesn't get in my way."

Opportunities to Use Skills and Abilities

Negative Comments:

"So now they want us to go into what they call multi-skilled cross training. I got to go to class to learn stuff I've been doing for years. Got to take a class in hydraulics and I've been fixing the stuff for fifteen years. It's just an insult. It's those damn engineers that think they know everything and don't have any common sense."

"These college kids don't know anything. They never get their hands dirty. I sent one for a box stretcher and he was gone all day. How can those people tell us if we are doing a good job."

"I went to the college of hard knocks. I've seen it all and done it all. These stupid testing programs are an insult. You get some jerk that has no experience telling me how I should do my job."

"No one can do it better that me. I'm the best at chemical handling. Where do these guys get off thinking that they know anything because they have a degree. Also, I've never seen a women do this job right."

Positive Comments:

"One of the best things management here has ever done was to take an experienced employee with them when they look for new equipment. We have to make this stuff run, we have to fix it, and we have to make it run flat out to capacity. I though it was smart of the management and engineers to take us along to see the vendors and get our opinion before the new equipment was bought."

"More money is the answer to everything. When management here sees that you can get the job done well, you can get an increase."

"My supervisor is okay. Not like at other places. When you are told to do more here, you get paid more."

"Hey, I'll get to buy the pickup truck I want in two months. Of course this is a good place to work."

Fair and Equitable Compensation

Negative Comments:

"For my job, we are so far below the market from what other companies pay that I would really like to quit. But I can't. I've been around here so long that I don't know how to look for another job."
"Nobody will hire someone my age. So I am stuck. In the handbook it says they'll pay competitive wages compared to other good companies. This must not be one of those good companies."

"Total compensation, who are they trying to kid? Why should I care how much benefits costs them? Besides, I haven't been sick a single day, so I didn't get anything and it didn't cost them anything."

"More money makes happier people. Why can't management understand that? They sure understand that more money for managers makes happier managers."

Positive Comments:

"I can get as much overtime as I want and then I make good money. When you get time and a half or double time then I'm getting what I'm worth."

"As long as everyone stays off my back, I can get the parts out and make decent money."

"This job has some danger and risk in it. So we get hazardous duty pay. Not too many people would do the kind of work I do even though the money is pretty good."

"I bought a new trailer because of the overtime. As long as I can work the overtime I'll stay here."

System 4 – Conventional

Trust Among Levels of Hierarchy

Negative Comments:

"The time I remember as the most negative was when they started this reengineering project. Then came downsizing, restructuring, flatting the organization, taking out levels of management and turning loose all those new college grads with MBA's and the consultants. Why didn't they ask us to find ways to save time and money? After all we know the place better than those outsiders."

"There's no longer any preventive maintenance programs here. Whenever we did complain we were told to run it 'till it breaks. It used to be that PM was built into production schedules. But now we're told it's not in the budget. I thought we were supposed to be maintenance technicians and not repairmen."

"We no longer have supervisors here. We have "Resource Coordinators." And there is only one on this shift for every one hundred machine operators. You can't even find them and have to wait 20 minutes if you use the beeper system. How is that supposed to improve productivity?"

"I'm a mechanic and my toolbox weighs 75 pounds and is on a cart, but the new rule says that we can't ride in the freight elevator. So I put the toolbox on the elevator and have to run upstairs and take it off on the other end. That is the stupidest rule I've ever seen. When I complained to the supervisor he said he had already told the operations manager about it, but he wouldn't change the rule."

"Management has created chaos and we don't like chaos. It seems that they change their mind every week about the direction of the company and the organizational structure. It's like a management best seller contest. Every time someone reads something new we have to try it. You can't count on anything and can't get the work done because you don't know what is going on or what the flavor-of-the-month is going to be."

Positive Comments:

"We have been given an employee handbook with all the policies and rules in it and its all there in black and white. You know what to expect from management because they follow their own rules and don't keep changing the rules to suit themselves.

"I used to be a supervisor, then they made me a 'Facilitator', then a 'Team Leader' and now I'm a 'Work Group Manager'. At least that tells my people who is in charge for a change."

"The new bidding system works better. Now seniority counts for something. Used to be all "merit", which is spelled 'B-U-D-D-Y'. Now we get points for years of service, number of skills you have and good attendance."

"Management has set a clear direction for us. The rules are clear and the work procedures are clear. Everyone gets trained the same way. We all know what is expected and can get our jobs done."

Freedom from Retribution

Negative Comments:

"If you don't watch your step and you make some little mistake it's going to come back to haunt you on your performance rating. If you get a bad rating, you can't bid on jobs. Seniority will not protect you if there is a layoff. Because managers know we can't trust them to be fair they put in this Alternative Dispute Resolution so they don't have to make a decision. I think that's their way to avoid a labor union cause they know they will get fired if one gets in."

"All those pep talks are worthless. What counts is how management really acts. They encourage participation and open communications then punish those who speak out the loudest. What do they want? Communication or silent robots?"

"The rules are always changing here. It's never consistent. How can you be a good employee and do the right things when you never understand what the rules are?"

"We learned from watching upper management. Whenever someone does not agree with the top dog, they seem to 'pursue other interests'. Well it all rolls down hill. If he treats people unfairly, then those he likes will do the same. Why would it be a surprise that we do not trust them?"

Positive Comments:

"The open door policy is good because it works here. There is a procedure you can use to make a complaint about something and you get an answer right away in writing. That way you know upper management knows what is going on."

"Everyone has to follow the rules, and they are right there in black and white in the handbook. Sometimes it can be a little tough and seem unfair, but that is how you should run a good organization – consistency."

"Management has encouraged questions and implemented a system called the 'Why' box. Anyone can ask a question through the process. Management responds in writing on the bulletin board and in the newsletter so that everyone sees the question and the answer. They don't avoid questions, they respond to them."

"I can tell my supervisor what I think. And he gives me an answer. That's all I ask for. I do not have to worry about retribution because he listens closely if anyone suggests that there may be retribution. He can keep a secret."

Communication and Feedback about Performance

Negative Comments:

"Management started this thing called a 360 review. I'm supposed to rate the people that I work with and they rate me. I don't spend much time with these people so how do I know what rating they deserve. Since they took away most of the supervisors, the ones that are left do not have time to know who is doing a good job and who is not. These 360's are supposed to help you develop and get along better. You fill out forms on two dozen people with page after page of rating scales. By the time you get to the third form, you give everybody a 4 on a 5-point scale just to get through with it."

"The 360 says you're supposed to guess how people are going to rate you on average. If your personal ratings are above that the counselor tells you have an ego problem. If you rate yourself lower than the group does, then the counselor says you have a poor self-image."

"I'm not really worried about 360's because management has never followed through on these kind of programs in the past and they will probably drop this one also."

"The design changes are made with the customer and we never know about it and then get blamed because the prints are not up to date."

"Sales promises everything to the customers and then expects us to follow through. They do not know the process and don't understand that sometimes their requests are impossible. And then we get blamed for the problem."

"We have a annual performance review system. The only thing you can count on is that the review will happen when your manager gets hammered for not getting them done. Annual means annual, not 8 months or 14 months – but annual."

"When I have a review with my supervisor, she just talks to me and then writes everything down afterwards. You can tell that there is no planning. No thought goes into the process. She just does it to get through with it "

"Management never thinks things through. Just like the last benefit changes. They announced everything and then couldn't answer any questions. They kept saying that the details aren't worked out and we'd be notified when the plans are finalized. The last time they did this it was 4 months after the start of the year before we knew how the plans had changed at the beginning of the year. It seems like every program they do is like that. How are we to know what is expected of us when they can't determine what the rules and expectations are before a new program is announced. They complain that we aren't 'flexible' enough but when you are trying to do a good job you need to know what is expected, not if you are 'flexible'."

Positive Comments:

"Awhile ago at the mine we had some other human resource managers from other places visit here to find out why we had such good attitudes. One guy asked what kind of communication program we have. I told him we don't have a program, we just talk. And we get a straight honest answer. And we give straight honest answers. We don't have popularity contests such as performance reviews. We just talk. Everyone knows where they stand. All that stuff the H.R. visitors were asking about: focus groups, 360's, performance appraisals, newsletters, big meetings – we don't do that. We just talk every day. We're here to work, not sit around in endless, time wasting team meetings talking about how we can communicate better."

"Since the cost crunch, they stopped the newsletter. That's fine with me. It was just a bunch of junior high stuff anyway."

"When I get on the elevator at work, I go to the third floor. The managers go to fifth floor. They always say hello and ask how things are going. Any problems that I am having they will listen to and then help me and my supervisor clear up the situation."

"When I meet with my supervisor, she is really prepared to discuss my job performance. She has facts, dates, figures and specific examples. That information and documentation helps me understand what I need to do differently and how I can improve. We're hired to do a good job and we should try hard to do just that."

"The management meetings here are okay. They actually listen and do not set their own agenda. They let us ask questions and they get us answers. Thank goodness that it is not one of those types of meetings where management says its an employee meeting then comes out with their agenda and tries to brainwash you."

Cooperation Among and Within Work Groups and Teams

Negative Comments:

"Our shift takes care of itself. We never see the people from the other shifts. We do our job and they do their job. Their supervisor does not make them clean up before they leave. Our supervisor makes us clean up for them and us. Then they say we are one big team. If that's true why do they talk about which shift is doing better? That doesn't sound like they want cooperation to me. Besides, when the managers in the front office do not cooperate, why should we? You always hear the rumors how they are playing games with the budget and worrying about how they look to the ivory tower people and not paying attention to what's going on within this place."

"The engineering prints are never correct and they won't cooperate when you bring it to their attention."

"Why are there no engineers on night shift? We were told that you could phone them at home. Sure! I called our engineer last week at 2 a.m. and got told where to go. Forget it. I told our boss about it and he said there was no way he was going to complain because they are engineers just like the top management. Can do no wrong!"

"I was told that it was important to get the ISO certification completed by the end of last year. We had to have it to be competitive. Ha! The engineers and production managers told me that they didn't have time to mess with it. When I asked my supervisor about the problem he just stated that I had to work it out and probably do it by myself. This seems a little strange if you want a cooperative effort and a successful program. Why can't all the priorities be the same for each department?"

"Our shift is the best. But those other shifts never cooperate with us. They leave everything in a mess and their supervisors don't care. When we asked our supervisor he just says he can't do anything about it. If housekeeping is important then everyone has to be made to live by the same standards."

"Ever since we got into teams and they set up rotating team leaders, there are no experienced supervisors to go to with a problem. Team leaders as just one of us hourly employees and they shouldn't be held responsible to know everything like a supervisor."

Positive Comments:

"When plans come down to us from upper management you can see that they took the time to think it through and have made sure that all departments know what they should be doing and how the whole program fits together. It's easy to cooperate because everything is lined out in detail. There are no gaps or bottlenecks, so we cooperate because the manufacturing process is carefully designed to get cooperation. You don't have to depend upon people's willingness to cooperate or put up with non-cooperation because the system takes care of that."

"Everyone lives by the same rules. Like at shift change, everyone cleans up and sets up for the person that follows you. It's not like that at other companies. You follow the rules and the expectations are clear. I think that helps to get the cooperation between shifts."

"Making the customer happy is everyone's job and that is made clear by management. When we have a problem we can go to anyone in the organization for assistance and there is never a lack of cooperation. It's good to know that all of us have the same priorities on a daily basis."

"I think that we get good cooperation because management has listened to us and then set up the rules and expectations for us so that we can understand them. And then they follow the same set of rules. You don't have to ask anyone for cooperation. It is just part of the way this place was designed."

"People are pretty tolerant here of differing views. I think that because we all listen and are listened to. Cooperation comes from knowing that your opinion was considered."

Freedom from Favoritism and Discrimination

Negative Comments:

"The main thing that upsets me is there is no longer any respect for seniority and experience. People, who have not been here long enough to find their way to the restroom, get picked on a job bid over experienced and seasoned people. When you ask management about that, they say we need new talent and new ideas. That's a slap in the face because it's saying that those of us who have been around can not have new ideas. When you ask why you did not get the job, you are told that you were qualified but someone else was more qualified. They don't tell you the truth because they are afraid they might get an age discrimination lawsuit."

"Why do managers and office people get to ignore the safety signs and walk through the shop without ear or eye protection?"

"If it is true that there is no discrimination here, then why are there no women in management roles? Every time I interview for a better position that has a manager title I'm told that someone else, generally from the outside, was better qualified. Yet, on non-managerial positions I always get selected."

"If our time is so valuable and everyone is living by the same rules, why do office people get to come in up to 10 minutes late or leave early and nothing is ever said to them. I'd get written up for that. And they get 15-minute breaks while we get 10 minutes. I think that is favoritism."

"The managers each have a private parking space with their name on it. We don't. We get to park in the back of the plant in the dirt. Even on weekends when no one is here from the office you can get disciplined for parking in the paved area even though no one from management will be here. That's favoritism in my book."

Positive Comments:

"There is no favoritism here because all the rules are clear. If someone gets out of line and starts harassing someone you just tell human resources about it and they put a stop to it. I don't mean there is never any discrimination here, but when it does happen, it gets fixed right away. It looks like management is trying to do the right thing and trying to make the policies work right. Maybe we had to have all these laws to make management do that, but at least they are doing it."

"Finally we can have radios in the shop like the office people have always had."

"Every since they made smoking anywhere on company grounds against the rules, the smokers don't cheat on their breaks. And they can't smoke in their offices any longer. That's fair for all."

"We used to have a problem with the buddy system here. It depended on who you knew and what neighborhood you lived in. That has stopped. Management put in a system where there are specific criteria that a person must meet to get a promotion. And it is well documented and known by everyone. Sure there is some questionable things that occur but it is working really well overall."

"Now everyone wears company shirts. Even the plant manager and all the rest of the big shots. The office clerical too. Even the new engineers get shirts. And we have our choice of color and style. It shows pride in the company and that even the managers are part of the team. It stopped all the nonsense about dress code and who could wear what."

Having a Positive Outlook for the Future

Negative Comments:

"The future is going to be just like the past. Nothing changes; management never sticks with anything that they start. They get all of those wild ideas from some management book and preach to us from their new bible. But, they don't do one thing that they just got through preaching. What is worse, we have to go to the training room and watch that videotape about the seven habits of highly effective people. Sounds to me like he's preaching his religion to us. He's a college professor that has never been in the real world. He is only effective at putting us to sleep. But if we put up with it, it's the last we hear about it until the next plant manager shows up."

"Since the British bought us all men in the office are wearing ties. Pretty soon they'll all be drinking tea."

"The management turns over so much nothing is consistent and nothing ever improves. You get some hot shot MBA engineer with wild ideas of change and he doesn't know anything about our operations. No, it's not going to get better. The cycle just repeats itself."

"I don't know where I stand anymore. We have all these new programs but no one got training. They took to heart the message that someone wrote about managing by chaos. We are a prime example of confusion and chaos. Why can't they learn from the past? Things don't work unless they are planned out and consistent."

"Why should I think that the future will be any better? Management just keeps messing with the new computers that they bought with new programs that do not work. This nonsense by consultants who have never worked in business is tearing us apart. Why can't management believe in its employees and stop having to get the outside experts 'advise'?"

Positive Comments:

"Why do I have a positive outlook about the future? I've thought about it a great deal. Over the years, most of what management said was going to happen, has occurred. Not all of it, but most of it. Management is not in a big rush. It doesn't have to be done by the end of the month or the end of the quarter. They take it one day at a time. But I believe in a saying that I read 'There is nothing so permanent as change'. The management here respects the traditions and history of this company and does not try to throw out everything from the past but builds' on it. So as far as I am concerned the future will be ok because the past has been okay."

"They respect us as individuals. We get a chance to participate in management brain storming sessions and they get to hear what we think. And they listen. It's the way a corporation should be run."

"The programs put in place for benefits and pay take care of my current needs. The policies and procedures can be understood and it is obvious that management believes in what they are saying. It makes the place good to work at because you know what to expect."

"This is a good place. Management has set a clear direction for the future and our supervisors have helped each of us to understand what our part is and what we must get done for the plans to happen. We're moving forward just a little at a time and now you can begin to feel and see the difference."

Opportunities to Use Skills and Abilities

Negative Comments:

"It used to be that you got ahead because of what you knew how to do. But lately management has changed all that. If you want an exempt job you have to have a college degree and it don't matter what the degree is in. What does a degree in some useless subject like history or literature have to do with being a supervisor? Three of us went to ask the human resources manager what a degree in nothing relevant has to do with supervision. He told us that it means you are trainable. Thanks a bunch."

"You can't get ahead anymore. People are just a commodity like a piece of equipment. The organization has become flat and there is nowhere to go. What has happened is that you work hard to keep your job knowing that you will never be rewarded any longer for hard work. As you skills and experience develop, the only thing you hear is 'that is what you get paid for'."

"I tried to get into the company college tuition reimbursement program. But I was told that the classes were not work related enough. So then I tried a different course of study. Then I was turned down because the class schedule would interfere with the normal working hours. How am I supposed to get ahead?"

"At my last place of employment I was certified in MIG and TIG welding. When I got here there was an opening a year later in the welding department. I bid for the job and wasn't even allowed to interview or test for the position. I have 15 years of experience at the other place. How can you get ahead if the management won't recognize experience gained outside of the organization. I think they recognize it when new managers apply to get hired into the company."

"I studied very hard when I was in school. Now that I completed the program, they do not seem to care. There is no more money.

I can't seem to get the promotions. What was all the talk about personal development? I did it and it didn't help. I might as well studied tap dancing instead of accounting."

Positive Comments:

"There is a lot of opportunities to use your skills and abilities here because we have a lot of training going on. When it was started it took some getting used to. But, they said everybody, including managers, must take the training. It started at 10 hours per year. Now it's up to 40 hours that is required. It is on company time. We do not have to work overtime to get the training. Then management put in skill based pay progression so that as you learn you could get a little bit more money. Not much more money. But it's like recognition. You get some money and a certificate. Then I can show my kids that their mother has to continue to go to school and that's why school is good for them. It took some getting used to, but when management starts early and is not in a big rush, you can get there eventually. That's why the tortoise won the race, not the hare."

"Management was smart. They offered the classes and people began to take them. Some of us work 12-hour shifts, some from 8 to 5 and others are on a rotational schedule. Management took all that into consideration and made the classes easy to fit into your schedule. And they went one step further – you got some C.E.U.'s for attending. That was great because it was like getting formal recognition for the education you were getting."

"When you show the initiative to learn a job well your supervisor really notices it. And then she will help you to get into a higher position if you want it. It's nice to know that hard work and dedication count for something. And if you are not interested in a higher position you get to help in more areas and demonstrate your knowledge."

"I like this place. Maybe the organization is flat and there are no promotions, but that doesn't matter. You get to learn a lot of things. And it's just this kind of learning that helps the company do better. I get the opportunity to learn about personnel issues and production both. I think this gives me a better understanding of the problems and consequently I learn how to make better solutions to problems. Management has encouraged this cross training and it is helping. Where else could I go and get the training that I am getting here. When management spends the time and money on developing its people you know that they are serious about the company's future and the individual's future."

Fair and Equitable Compensation

Negative Comments:

"This new pay for performance is an insult. You are going to get a merit rating and if its good enough you get a raise. The managers say its going to motivate us. But it's an insult because that means they do not think we are working hard already. Do those guys up there really think that 1% more than average is going to get people working harder and going faster? They got to be smoking something. They may be kidding themselves but they aren't fooling us."

"Human resources policy changes are just posted on the board and never discussed in our monthly meetings. This helps to keep everything about the pay system a secret. When I brought this up in a meeting, I was told it was my responsibility to read the bulletin board every day and that is all I needed to know. How does that fix the secrecy problem? She won't give me a copy of the notice or any information about the system."

"The point system for absence makes no sense. Why don't they count attendance instead? Why does everything have to be so negative around here? They should give us credit for good attendance."

"You can accumulate paid days off for good attendance and save up to 250 days to use when you need them. But when you retire they won't let you cash them in, so what people fixing to retire try to do is take the days a few at a time so they won't lose them. But if you do that you get written up for bad attendance and could be fired just before you retire."

"I've been here for sixteen years and I'm still not at the top rate. When I asked my supervisor about it, he said I still have room for improvement. But I'm only 8 cents from the top. That doesn't make any sense.

Positive Comments:

"Why do I trust mangers to pay fairly? It's because the pay grades and the minimums and the maximums and the timing are all posted on the bulletin board. So are the names of the companies that they use in their pay survey. We are told that we are paid equal to or better than the other companies and when you look at the overall averages of the other companies you can see where we fit in. Once a year on the same date we get a cost of living adjustment and we stay in line with the other companies. Also management eliminated a bunch of the pay classifications and ranges to make it easier to understand and less work for the supervisors. In other words – come to work, do your job and you don't have to worry about it. There are no secrets or surprises."

"Management has a philosophy to share when times are good. In our 401(k) program, we can get an extra 2% matching if the year was good. Management can only get their full bonus if we get our extra 2%. So when the business has done well we all share. Not the same amount but at least everyone gets something."

"I don't have a problem with the pay system. You know up front what your supervisor is going to do. The expectations are clear. If you meet them, you get the maximum raise. If you don't, you get nothing. And if you keep getting bad ratings, you get fired."

"I like the fact that the pay program is competitive and provides me with a good living. But we have these extra things like ESOP and 401(k), which help me to prepare for the future. I mean colleges are not cheap anymore and these programs help me plan for my children's education."

Value System 5 — Competitive

Trust Among Levels of Hierarchy

Negative Comments:

"The most significant problem I have experienced in trusting higher management is their excessive focus on the bottom line. We have been involved in writing mission statements, vision statements and corporate values that talk about the customers, vendors, the community etc. But the bottom line is the bottom line."

"I understand that we have to make profits but I would appreciate it if the corporate executives would simple be brutally honest and state that it all has do with stock prices, stock options and the price/earnings ratio. Stop this other rhetoric."

""Ethics is spelled M-O-N-E-Y. If you can make it for them, you stay employed. If not, you find another job."

"They always make the subtle promises of a brighter future. So I do what they say. Then when the project is done they somehow forget about the promises."

"I've always done what they have asked of me. Not once did I ever question what they said or asked. But what do I get out of it? Nothing. No you can't trust them."

Positive Comments:

"I think I can have a positive attitude and trust top management because I understand exactly how they think, because I think the same as they do. So I'm just going to ignore all that hype about mission and values because it's all about money, isn't it? Besides we have a stock option plan and a bonus plan and one of these days in the future I'll be in those plans. That's why I am here. So I guess it's not that I trust the managers as individuals but I know how the game is played. And I am here to win."

"Trust us only skin deep. Face the facts, man. We are all here to win. The prize is material stuff; houses, cars, vacations, recognition, awards, etc. You need to accept that fact. Trust is siding with whoever can do me the most good at that time. The problem is that upper management doesn't remember who their friends are when the game is over, but that's okay because there are always some winners and many losers."

"Sure I trust management. They know what I want and as long as they deliver I'll be here doing whatever they ask."

"All management can be trusted within this organization. Look at them. They are rich. They got it all and will get more and that's okay. What is the point of being in management if there are no rewards. After all we take all the risks."

"Employees just do not understand management and what we are trying to accomplish. Sure we get big rewards for our efforts but it does provide them jobs. Too bad they do not understand that. We can be trusted because without our work they would have no jobs."

Freedom from Retribution

Negative Comments:

"There is an 'in' group and an 'out' group here and if you don't get close to the big bosses or play golf with them, or drive the right car, then they aren't going to notice you. The trouble is I don't like golf and I don't like the sports utility vehicles that they drive. But if you don't play the game you better CYF because there could be consequences. It's never blatant. You get told that your job has been eliminated and you need to pursue other interests. They just bribe you to quit. So there may be retribution, but as usual they think money will make everything right."

"They think they are too smooth to let any one believe there is retribution. When they decide to get rid of someone they just start looking for excuses. Things like "not a team player" or getting consensus from co-workers that you somehow do not fit in. It's always made up in their minds but they get people to believe it."

"It all starts as a new fad. This group has every one take a personality test to see how they will best fit into the organization. When the results come back they use the results to show why certain people should be retained and others let go. It's not on ability but whether you are able to kiss up to the right people."

"They practice all types of retribution. I've never seen management practice real discrimination because there are legal consequences which can cost money and people could get fired. But with retribution there isn't any monetary or job security consequences for the good game players."

"When management decides you are great for a special project, they are really saying 'we want you to take on this project so that we have a reason to get rid of you.' Everyone that has taken on special projects has been fired. But management always has an excuse."

Positive Comments:

"You asked me why I don't believe there is retribution in this company? The reason is that I am good and they know that I am good. And I see to it that the customers and top management knows who I am. If you spend some time schmoozing when the big guys come to town, there is always somebody up there who knows who I am so that if I get crossways with my immediate boss, nothing is going to happen. He knows that I have connections above him."

"There is no retribution here. Everyone who has been involved in the game knows how to play. And they know all the things that have happened that were not right, legally or ethically. So, we all keep our jobs. They are afraid to fire anyone because of the potential consequences of information getting out. But that is okay. If keeps me employed and enjoying the benefits of being highly paid."

"When you think of retribution, I think that it is possible towards us managers. We have the tough job. That's why we get the rewards. All those other people just come in and do repetitive tasks. We have to think and be good at beating the competition, whether internal or external. But we are not forgiven for our mistakes. They are. But that's okay. That's why I can afford my BMW – I am not in that lower class group of favorites around here."

"There is no retribution. Anyone who believes that is wrong. It costs money to be involved in retribution. I'm good at my job and I get stock options and a bonus. Those people who believe that there is retribution, they are just jealous because they aren't good enough yet and may never be."

"The claims about retribution are all false. It's only a perception that people turn into a make-believe reality. We have to run the business. The good people get the breaks, all others don't. They are just envious of those of us who are smarter, better educated and smoother at doing our jobs."

Communication and Feedback about Performance

Negative Comments:

"I don't like to hear about the negative stuff. There is a communication gap within this organization. It's against the unwritten rules to ask questions of upper management. Everything must go up and down the chain-of-command. By the time it gets to you all you hear is your boss's interpretation and it may not be exactly what the top management wanted. It may not even be straight talk from the top. And then, there is this performance review where you get a rating but it has nothing to do with your pay raise. So what's the point of it? And the latest gimmick is the 360. All my so-called peers are going to rate me on performance and personality. So I guess I'll have to play along with the popularity contest."

"Management started this brilliant program on downsizing. If they had been paying attention to begin with, the downsizing wouldn't be necessary. The process of determining who goes and who stays is a dart board game. They use this as the excuse of getting rid of people who speak honestly and those have consistently been poor performers. Downsizing was just the ticket they needed for doing what they were afraid to do – talk honestly to people. Now they can blame the program."

"Honesty is as rare here as on a used car lot. Management wants their programs to do the talking. Not one of them can look an employee straight in the eye and give an honest answer. How can you run an organization like that long term?"

"Our performance evaluation system is a good example of management's inability to talk honestly to people. Everyone, including the dead weight, gets an increase."

"Performance issues are never dealt with. Then management always states that there are extenuating circumstances. That's bull. They dream up the circumstances to avoid doing what they are paid to do. By not addressing the problem, it just demoralizes the rest of us."

Positive Comments:

"The time I had the most positive attitude about communication was when upper management awarded me the trophy for top salesman of the year at the annual banquet. Now let me tell you why I felt good about that. You see, everybody knew what I had achieved and I could take that trophy home, show it to my spouse and kids and that's a good feeling. It's nice to know you are good and everyone else to know that you are good. And it can go on the mantle with my other trophies. You know that second place is only the first place loser."

"When management gives out this award for innovation it can be a real boost. I got it for my part in some human resources issues. Of course, a couple of others received the same award, one was drunk at the party and the other wasn't even there through the process."

"Management always knows who is contributing and who is not. Those of us, like me, that did well last year, were told in front of the whole organization by the President about our achievements. The communication is good here."

"Communication is excellent. My confidants within the company always tell me about what is happening. If something isn't going the right way I have time to make adjustments so the outcome is right."

"I believe that communication is good. We don't have to bother with those stupid reviews any longer. If you get a good bonus, you did well. If, not, you did badly. The communication is the type that we need – put your money where your mouth is."

Cooperation Among and Within Work Groups and Teams

Negative Comments:

"Why are there teams? There are always stars on every team. Management wants us to be a team but they forget about the stars. It's like a communist philosophy. Everybody has to be the same. So the idea is to cooperate or at least have management think that they have teamwork. You just use all the buzz words and carry that vision statement in your wallet and make sure you work it into conversations and your status reports."

"Cooperation is state of mind. Everyone knows it's a competitive world and you have to fight to win. You only get cooperation through bribery. Management is way off base thinking that cooperation is going to help anything."

"I will cooperate if it's required by the boss, but what a waste of time. I can't do my job when I'm trying to help some other dufus get his project done. It's really a waste of my time."

"Teamwork is one of our values that management talks about. What a joke. They compete with each other, then preach to us about teamwork. They should try and set an example first."

Positive Comments:

"This idea about team work coming from our leadership team at the top gives us a new paradigm to work with. As long as this organization is a winning team and continues to equal or exceed customer expectations, then good team players are going to share in the rewards. You have to believe that life is a game, business is a game, love is a game – but never forget that the goal is to win."

"Team work has made my job easier. I can get others to help me do the work and then I can put the project together really fast."

"Working with R&D has been very valuable. I can now tell my clients about new developments before anyone else gets a chance and beat them to the punch. I think team work and cooperation should be encouraged."

"I love this team concept. I can give my team members the articles and books I've read and ask them to read them. Then when we work on a project they all seem to agree with me about everything we discuss. It's really made my job easier."

"Cooperation is higher now than ever before. I've had to fire a lot of people due to downsizing. The group I have left is just excellent. Whenever something needs accomplished, they'll work endless hours to get it done. I think because there are fewer of us, cooperation has become more important."

Freedom from Favoritism and Discrimination

Negative Comments:

"There is a pecking order around here. And where you fit in the hierarchy determines what kind of perks you get. Some people get company cars, company credit cards, reserved parking, first class airline tickets, offices with windows, etc. It all has to do with status. I am as good at doing my job as they are at doing theirs so why do they get all that stuff and I don't. A lot of times when there is meetings and conferences, the marketing people get to go and spend company money but the rest of us stay home and make money for the company. If that sounds like I envy those people the answer is 'Hell, yes I do'."

"Discrimination is not existent here, but favoritism is. If you are liked by a certain white-haired individual and play golf, you've got it made in the shade. Or if you buy Amway products from a certain person, you'll never get a bad review. It is all over the plant, but you got to ignore it or it will eat you up."

"Favoritism is the CEO's occupation. He pouts if he doesn't get what he wants. And sometimes what he wants is just a plausible excuse as to why the organization is doing so poorly. If you can't deliver, you'll pay. The first step is to not get invited to the next management retreat."

"I've never seen discrimination. I see favoritism all the time. I experience it. Just because I don't like fishing and outdoor activities I've become a social outcast. I thought I was hired to do a job well but I found out that I couldn't' get what is due me because I don't enjoy certain activities."

Positive Comments:

"I have never felt that there was favoritism or discrimination here. The people who produce get the rewards, the promotions and recognition. If others think that there is, it's just their excuse for a lack of motivation. What do they think - that the world owes them a living? They can get off their dead asses and get with the program. If people believe that there is favoritism and discrimination they are just under-achievers."

"Things are fine here. People get these crazy ideas about what is happening and it's just not true. They just are envious of us and have to have some excuse as to why they aren't in the power group."

"I've never seen any favoritism or discrimination since I came here two years ago. I was brought in from the outside as the new VP and people just resent that the job wasn't handed to them. I believe that if you really analyze the situation, no one here was ready for the responsibility and new blood was needed. They just don't understand."

"Well, we don't have any suits filed against us so there isn't discrimination. If there was favoritism I think people would talk openly about it. You know we really encourage people to talk openly. We use round table meetings and focus groups, etc. No one has ever stated in those meetings that we have discrimination."

Having a Positive Outlook for the Future

Negative Comments:

"Ever since management downsized there is no opportunity for promotion here. Since they chopped rungs out of the ladder there is nowhere to climb. If the organization is downsizing and not growing what is the point of staying here? That's why I'm floating my resume with corporate recruiters. I mean, if this place is not going to be fast track, I'm out of here."

"My boss doesn't recognize talent when it bites him. I've done more than anyone else could in the department and yet he doesn't trust me with the big accounts. He says I need "seasoning." That sounds like something you get when you get old. If he can't recognize a winner, then I'm sure that the competition will."

"I've had it with this organization. I've done everything they wanted and even developed some new products that they didn't have before and yet they don't give me the promotion. What crap. My boss doesn't appreciate all that I can do. What am I going to do? Lay low and let the alleged lady make a fool out of herself."

"All I ever want is an answer why I am not allowed to participate in the bonus program and company car program. Is it the job or is it me? Why don't they give me a company car?"

113

Positive Comments:

"Since our restructuring there may be fewer slots in mid-management but they keep adding to division and corporate staff. The overhead groups are growing. It's like an inverted pyramid. So I am targeting my future at headquarters, not down here in the lower floors of the organization. There is always opportunities when you understand how the system works."

"Management always recognizes contributors. Promotions are based upon talent. The golf games, outings and country club are not for seeking favoritism. They are an opportunity to demonstrate social skills that are needed to augment one's professional knowledge. This organization knows the value of social skills and so the future looks good."

"The future is just a snap shot in a small time frame. The organization changes and the needs of the organization change. Those people who complain that ability is not recognized are wrong. Ability means having flexibility to change with the needs of the organization. Competition is not standing still. Just because you have a set of professional skills that are good today doesn't mean that they are valuable tomorrow. This organization has all types of future potentials for those with the 'flex'abilities."

Opportunities to Use Skills and Abilities

Negative Comments:

"Its tough to work here when you have an engineering degree. Since the bean counters took over and put in that centralized, computerized control system there is no room to maneuver. The thrill is gone. You can't wheel or deal. You can't do people a favor. What is the point of knowing how to do a lot of stuff if a computer with a green eyeshade is calling all the shots? They talk to us about being entrepreneurs within the enterprise but entrepreneurs are independent of controls and run their own show."

"You can't do anything today. All the laws, government interference and labor unions have taken all the spirit out of business. I used to be able to manage everything I touched. Now there are laws against it. No, the business climate has changed and the opportunity to be successful has vanished."

"You can't demonstrate skills and abilities here. All that is allowed is ass kissing. That's all that is appreciated. No one cares how good you are, just how well you play the game and if you are not a good player you are dead."

"The use of peoples' skills is impossible. They are more interested in credentials than performance. Since I don't have an MBA I never get the opportunities to get the good projects."

"All these guys want is to make themselves look good. So our good work can be viewed as bad work if it doesn't please their self-image. You don't dare to demonstrate true ability for fear that it may be better than what the powers-in-charge could do."

Positive Comments:

"You know, in a lot of companies they tell you have freedom to make mistakes – well that is true here. The CEO actually practices what he preaches. So the idea of acting like you own the company and taking risk is true. It's not just one of those hot new concepts coming from the fly-by-night consultants. In other words, the great thing about this company is that you can stretch to the limit of your abilities."

"I have a rare opportunity. Management will give you the freedom to do your job within certain guidelines. If you get the results, then you get more. If you don't, then you get to try again to win. It's a good situation."

"Some of the new management ideas are great. It gives you an opportunity to try new concepts that get the people in the organization to do the right thing. It also gives me an opportunity to further develop my skills so that I know about the latest trends in business."

"I can not understand why people complain about the change within the organization. Every new program allows an opportunity to improve your value to the company. Some people just don't understand that change is the enabler of ingenuity and we all benefit from that."

Fair and Equitable Compensation

Negative Comments:

"I went to see human resources to find out about the maximum on my pay range. Am I in the bottom or top quartile? How much more room is there to make money here? Maybe it is so secretive because I'll find out I'm underpaid and just quit or that I'm so close to the top that I'll never get another raise. If you don't understand how the compensation plan works, how do you know if you are getting what you are worth?"

"Our plan doesn't work. Last year I exceeded my goals and since someone else exceeded theirs even further they got the vacation trip and I didn't. The company says that you will get rewarded if you do well, but it didn't happen for me."

"These compensation and incentive plans are too strict. How was I supposed to know that one customer would close their doors and leave my territory short on total sales? It wasn't my fault that they closed but I get punished. The system should be a guide only and discretion should come into play on situations like mine."

"It isn't fair that I produce a lot more sales than the other areas and yet I can only get the same amount of commission as the other reps. If my territory generates the most, then I should get the most. These systems do not take into account your total contribution, just those parts to make everyone happy. Who cares about the rep with a small territory? If they can't grow it, it should not hold down my earnings."

"If we really had merit pay some people in this room would get nothing."

Positive Comments:

"It's easy to find out if I am paid right or not. I just look in the annual pay survey of professional journals and there it is. Or I can feel out some of those ads in the New York Times or even get it off the Internet. So, if I'm paid right for my experience and organizational level, then management is being fair. If not, then there are other opportunities out there. Now when it comes to incentives, as long as it is done on a percentage of your base rate and recognizes outstanding performance, it is a good add on, but it doesn't make up for a low base rate. After all management does call it 'at risk'.

"The system is fair as long as I get what I deserve. Who cares about the others in the department? This is not a team thing. I am responsible for the outcomes and I should get paid for the outcome. They do that around here. It's pure percentage pay out base rate and that's how it should be."

"This is a great place to work. I get paid on commission. So I do not have to worry if my co-worker is doing great or not. That's her problem. As long as I get my fair share I stick around. If they don't pay me my fair share then I'll leave."

"Compensation is a broad subject. It covers cars, salary, bonuses, and use of the condo, use of the company plane among other things. You have to look at the whole picture to

117

make sure you are getting the right rewards. The CEO had access to all of these when she was in sales. If I can get access to all of these, then I'm paid fairly and am on the right track to success and proper compensation."

Value System 6 – Compassionate

Trust Among Levels of Hierarchy

Negative Comments:

"Let me share with you my feelings about trust among people in this organization. What you see in this company is the same thing you see in all parts of our society. There are the 'haves' and the 'have nots'. And the 'haves' have it all and they still want more. And crumbs trickle down to the rest. What it's all about is pure greed. Some people in our nation have more than they know what to do with, but they give nothing to the people. Same thing happens in this corporation. The top people get more and more in bonuses and the rest of us get less and less in our paycheck. We have all these people around here that management calls 'temporaries' but some of them have been here for years and there is more and more of them in the company. They get paid half of what we do and don't get our benefits. It's just the modern version of slave labor."

"I work in R&D. I know that management is only interested in money and does not care about anything else. When we develop products, there are a variety of choices on the chemicals we use. Some are environmentally friendly but cost more. Our management is not interested in the environment because they always elect the cheap way out and that is the chemicals that do the most harm. If they can't make the right decision on environmental issues, they can not be trusted. They just want more money."

"Management doesn't care about people at all. They think that downsizing and reengineering are the answers to everything. They never stop to consider the impact on people's lives or their families. We all are good people and they treat us like we were horrible people by laying some of us off."

119

"I can tell you for a fact that management can not be trusted. I do volunteer work with older citizens. They need a lot of help. I requested a small donation to help an older couple get their house painted and management said it wasn't in the budget. Now when I look at the parking lot they all have new cars and they are expensive cars. But paint for an older couple is not in the budget? You can tell they are motivated by greed."

"They all got training on something called the seven habits. It's funny that none of the habits talk about relationships with people. They took it to make points with headquarters. They learned nothing about true leadership."

Positive Comments:

"The management of our company really does believe in people. We all get the same benefits. Everyone is salaried, so they get paid even when they can not work. And if somebody has a major personal problem in his or her family, management shows compassion. And when we get bonuses for having a good year every person gets the same dollars. I mean even the plant manager gets the same money I do. We all worked equally hard at our jobs. And another thing, the managers treat us as equals and all know us by our first name. We all eat in the same lunch room, share the same parking lot and share the same entrance."

"Management cares about the people in this company. We have all been here a long time and management respects that. They don't try to control us. They allow us to do our jobs and then decide what projects will be fun to work on. We've had a lot of good ideas developed into neat products because management didn't try to tell us what to work on."

"My group all believes that management is okay. We discussed it in our last monthly meeting and came to that consensus. Everyone agreed. They let us take the time off we need to be with our families and to help on community projects. They even encourage it and sometimes you will see some of management helping out on volunteer work. Yeah, they do care. Sometimes they have to do unpopular things but overall they are a good group."

"When her son was hurt in a car accident some of us took time off work to help care for him at her home. Management didn't mind. They even paid for us to be there as long any one person was not gone for more than one day a week. Most management groups would never do that. Our managers saw the need for personal assistance and that Rita could not afford the help, so they allowed us to help. They really care."

Freedom from Retribution

Negative Comments:

"If you speak up in support of your peers, you might get labeled as a trouble maker or if management thinks that you are an inside labor organizer trying to bring justice within in the organization you can get fired. I've noticed that when people trying to stand up for their rights suddenly are treated as if they do not exist. I've seen a department head turn his back on me just because I asked a question in a meeting. They just want to freeze me out. I am not going to quit because that would be abandoning my friends."

"Our group has seen a number of examples of retribution. Everyone should be treated with respect and not be judged by their opinions. Yet management will always make a big deal out of some one expressing themselves openly. We have that right under the constitution. And it's only fair that we get an opportunity to speak openly about any issue. Just because we do not like the opinions of others is no reason to get upset. Management has no understanding of, or tolerance for, the beauty of diversity."

"Management really blew it with our group. All we wanted to do was set up a means by which people could sign up for different activities that would help the community. We even had a list of speakers from various agencies ready to come in and talk to us. And what did management do? Told us we had to do it on our own time. They really don't care about anything but themselves."

"They did it again. They always give money to things they like the flight museum. What good does that do? It doesn't help any one. It just makes management look good to the big wigs in the town. They never budget money for the poor people in the community. When HACAP offered to supply disadvantaged people to assist in our office areas, management wouldn't do it. They thought it would be too disruptive. Well what about those disadvantaged people? They need something to make them feel good about themselves."

Positive Comments:

"We don't have to fear retribution here because management put in this peer review system which means if one of us gets in trouble or gets discriminated against, we can pick our peers to be on the panel to hear the dispute. Of course management gets two people from their side, but its like being judged by a jury of your peers, not trying to prove to a judge you are not guilty. Since management has empowered the people here instead of keeping all the power in their own hands, we don't need to worry about it. The peer review panel can correct it by overruling management."

"It's nice to have a management group you know is concerned about all employees equally. When we have our monthly meetings, we can point out the things that need done to make people's life easier and management responds. They put in the flextime system just because of our suggestions. Now people can come and go as they please just as long as they get the work done during the week. Now people can attend other family functions and community projects without having to worry about your job."

"We all get the same consideration around here. Just because someone is different or may express feelings that are not popular, it's okay. We all get the personal respect that we deserve as human beings. And management does not bother people who are different."

Communication and Feedback about Performance

Negative Comments:

"You know some of the things that management does do not make sense. We talk about teamwork, empowerment and self-directed teams but they still evaluate individuals. It looks like another management sham to please the executives. It's like management complains about the grapevine and they try to stop the rumors. But they haven't figured out that that you can't stop people from talking. You can't stop people from speaking the truth."

"Management is always talking about the accomplishments of various individuals. Don't they realize that here in R&D we all work together? None of these things would have happened if we hadn't all been participating. Why do they think that all good comes from a single individual? It doesn't. It comes from collective efforts and the group efforts."

"I could not believe what I was hearing at the management dinner at the country club. Our president stood there and told everyone how well the sales rep in Maine was doing. He doesn't realize that it took a lot of R&D effort to make that business happen. Everyone in R&D contributed somehow. It's not fair when management doesn't see the effort put forth by everyone."

"I can't believe this management group. They tell us that we are all on the same team. Yet, when I get on the elevator to go up to my floor I hope that no one from management is on it. If they are, they just look at the floor and wait for me to get off. They don't talk to any of us, they don't look at any of us – they act as if the group has some exotic disease. Don't they know that we are all people, just like them?"

Positive Comments:

"Around here you can walk up to anyone in management – even if they do not know you and ask them about why decisions have been made. And they will take time to explain it right then. None of this business of "I'll look into it" or "I'll get back to you." It gives you the feeling that your questions and ideas are respected. As long as there is feedback about how well someone is doing his or her job, we don't need any official forms. The people in our work group talk to each other when we need help. We talk about what the person needs to do to do better, but we have respect for that person's feelings so we don't go too far."

"The 360 feedback process really works well here. The group gets to evaluate the individuals. And you know, we are all pretty good. With this new process we all get a turn at saying something good about everyone. It makes us feel good about each other and we know that our collective comments are helping that person to. It was a good idea to put in that process."

"Management has done some wonderful things for us. They match the contributions that we make to community groups that help disadvantaged individuals. That way the people are getting more money to assist in the things that are important to their lives. I think this management group really does care. Then they post information on the bulletin boards and the company newsletter about the various organizations and what we as a group are doing so that everyone knows."

Cooperation Among and Within Work Groups and Teams

Negative Comments:

"The time when I feel the most upset about cooperation is when another team is unfairly criticizing our group – like when the group we pack the kits for loses a part and then blames us. Or they break a unit and then blame us for poor quality work. Our supervisor knows it wasn't our fault. But, she can not do anything about it because her boss tells her to get the teams together and work it out. And it just doesn't work that way."

"When I feel bad about this organization is when management preaches cooperation then creates a competitive environment. Competition is not good. People get hurt. You do not need winners and losers. You need everyone to work together and help those who may not do as well as you."

"Everything around here is on a business plan with a timetable. Those timetables are horrible. Why does management think that you can assign a timetable to everything? It's like they always expect results. Well sometimes you have to go at the pace that is best for the group. And if management doesn't like it, too bad!"

"Our supervisor doesn't understand that people have various needs and that you can not overlook these special needs when looking at the work that needs to be accomplished. Everyone wants to work together. But our supervisor breaks us into groups and then makes us compete for getting the projects done. How can you have cooperation when you are competing with your own co-workers? That is crazy. If she wants us to communicate and cooperate we should all be on the same team, working on the same project and making sure that individual needs are met to help everyone do a better job."

Positive Comments:

"Our new manager put a stop to all the bitching and back biting that was going on. Some people picking on other people because of the color of the skin, or the neighborhood they live in, or they don't speak English very well. But that is all stopped. He made it clear that anyone of us who does not treat everybody with respect and a cooperative spirit they would not be working here."

"Our supervisor is a wonderful person. He recognizes that each of us is different and we each have our own little quirks. So he works with us so that the group can perform better."

"My group and my supervisor are excellent to work with. I have experience in counseling so when someone has a problem I am allowed to use my skills with that person so that the whole group can benefit."

Freedom from Favoritism and Discrimination

Negative Comments:

"The management put these non-discrimination equal opportunity statements in the handbook and on the bulletin board and it's signed by the president of the company but it didn't stop it. It's not as blatant racism and sexism as it used to be but it is still there. It's subtler. I think that they did it because they are afraid of lawsuits and the lawyers scared them. I don't think they are really sincere. There are just concerned because it could cost them their bonus."

"Have you ever spent time in our cafeteria. Management allows people to joke about one another. I mean, they think it is okay to make fun of people then they aren't doing their jobs right. Someone could get his or her feelings hurt. And if they do, then they probably won't feel like working with the group. You need to be careful about what is stated to people to make certain their feelings aren't hurt. Happy people are cooperative people."

"Management doesn't practice what they preach. They put out this employee rights and values statement. Not one item in it is followed. They talk about everyone having the opportunity to excel to the best of their abilities. That's not true. It depends upon who you are and whom you know. No one in our group is allowed to work up to their abilities. Management always determines who will work on which assignments. And the assignments are based upon favoritism."

"There is always discrimination. How many women are in management? I speak for the whole group when I say that management only wants women around here to look at. They treat us all as if we don't have a brain. And the work assignments are based upon sex. They think we can not do the heavier work. It's pure discrimination."

Positive Comments:

"I don't have a problem because management doesn't tolerate sexism and racism in this company. Period. The people who kept it up or their managers or supervisors were warned once and fired the second time."

"The supervisor we have has really made an effort to assign the jobs equally to everyone. She uses a rotational system of assignment so that everyone gets to do all the jobs equally and no one is favored."

"Management lets everyone have an equal opportunity to train in any area. The company has these training programs for all of the groups. And anyone can attend. That way, if you are interested in something else, or if the group wants to learn about something else, we all have the opportunity."

Having a Positive Outlook for the Future

Negative Comments:

"I find it's very difficult to have a positive outlook about the future because management would rather pollute and pay the fine instead of fixing the problem. It's like safety. We have to have an accident before they do anything about it. It's been this way for years. Management does not give a damn about the people or the environment. They think that writing a check takes care of it all."

"I don't see a future for me here any longer. Management said that it is cheaper to move our operations that use chemicals to overseas facilities than to follow government regulations. They care more about continuing poor practices than keeping people employed."

"Things never change. They are just greedy. When we have an opportunity as a company to do something nice for people or the community the management always finds a way to get out of helping. They just don't care about anything but the money. With that attitude, things can never get better."

"They do not care about us any more. They stopped all the activities where we could meet with fellow employees. You know you can meet interesting people much different than yourself when you attended. Now there is no opportunity. And management talks about learning diversity. That'll never happen here in the future."

Positive Comments:

"We have the most wonderful thing here. You can have time off with pay to participate in helping people who need help. We get two days per year for helping do community service. Last year our manager suggested that anyone who would like to meet on Thursday morning to help out with the cooking and cleaning and serving Thanksgiving dinner at the shelter of the homeless would be most welcome, but we only got the paid holiday. But that is good."

"Our personnel department organized a group of people to go out and paint the houses of retired and disadvantaged people. Every year we do three houses. And the company pays for the material and pays us for the time we spend there. It's good to work for a company that is concerned about the community and the people within the community."

"Our management team goes beyond United Way. They allow people in the organization to coordinate community projects right from work. I've been involved in a number of organizations like boy scouts and was able to use the company equipment and do the work on company time. It's a good place to work."

Opportunities to Use Skills and Abilities

Negative Comments:

"I feel that I am a very creative person. I have a lot of creative activities off the job, but management does not seem to care. They only like creativity that will make some money. There is a lot of stuff we could do such as teaching English to employees from other countries. There are a lot of really talented people in this company that could do so many good things if they have the support from management. Every time something comes up management says that can not accept the legal risks if something goes wrong. They tell us that they are not here for social work and if we want to do this stuff we should go out into the community and do it. When is there time for that when they work us twelve hour shifts and make us work on weekends?"

"What I think is that management does not care what a person can really do. They just put you in a box and keep you there. All of us here are very creative people and can do much more than we are doing now. But management expects to stay with the business plan and to focus on timetables. How can you be creative by the clock? How can you experience new discoveries when you have to follow a plan?"

"I am a qualified EMT. And I could teach our supervisors to be good first responders. I could also put together a safety program that would benefit all the employees in the company. But since I am in customer service, they won't let me. I would think that helping other people when they are hurt would be more important than filling out the forms for the sales department."

Positive Comments:

"The times when I feel the greatest satisfaction is when I know I have used my skills to help a customer solve a problem. After all, this is the customer service team and those who work here enjoy the opportunity to be creative and do whatever is necessary to take care of the customer. Our management has not only permitted this, but they have encouraged us to go as far as we think is right. The motto here in this company is 'Use your own best personal judgement'.

"I feel good about this organization. The human resources department put together a skills inventory that shows all the training and experience that a person has. Then, as the needs arise, whether it's work related or for community activities, they do a computer search and contact the people with the required skills so that we have an opportunity to use those skills."

"Our group thinks that management is interested in the skills of people. Every year the management talks about the things that are going on and what they would like to accomplish within the organization and within the community. Then they ask for volunteers to assist in these areas.

Fair and Equitable Compensation

Negative Comments:

"How can I believe management when they talk about teamwork but do not pay everybody on the team the same amount. When we started into teamwork, they didn't get rid of the old pay for performance. Not only that, they have some bell shaped distribution curve, which allows only a few to get the top rating, and some have to get the bottom rating. Just because someone can't do the job quite as well doesn't mean they should get paid less. After all, they need the money as bad as someone else."

"Management put in this gainsharing plan. But everybody believes that they are messing with the accounting. No one can understand the system so it becomes another manipulative gimmick that exploits the people."

"It's the same old 'have and 'have not' game around here. Management keeps getting more and more and we get less and less. The gap grows larger. The program they put in gives us a percentage increase. Well, that's not fair. The cost of everything goes up for everyone at the same rate. It's not fair that 3% for one person is more money than for someone else."

Positive Comments:

"Pay is not really a problem, because after you learn to do the job we all get paid the same. That way money does not become a barrier in helping and working with one another. Every year management keeps us up with the cost of living so you never lose ground. But it's the fairness of equal pay that is most important. That makes it okay."

"Management pays our group well. They put in a program where we can earn extra income if the group does a good job. Last year we all got a $500 check. We know that if the group does well then we will all share the same in making our goals."

"The management is on the same bonus program and benefit program as all employees. So we know that when pay and benefits impact us, it will impact the management group in the same way."

Value System 7 – Conscious

Trust Among Levels of Hierarchy

Negative Comments:

"It's tough to have fairness and confidence in management when management has no confidence in itself. Look at all the controls we have; auditing, accounting, reviews, budgets, etc. They like to talk about planning but it is really about controlling from the top with a computer that has to be feed so much information to upper management so they can know everything and micro-manage everything. You can't get your job done. That's not trust – that's control with a Pentium processor."

"How can you trust management when management doesn't trust you. They place more confidence in the consultants and contract people than they do in employees. When I've come up with new concepts for review, management must have the consultants give their stamp of approval first before I can proceed. If they do not trust their own judgement or that of the employees, how can I trust them?"

"Our new president goes around with a ruler and measuring how high the venetian blinds are from the window sill. The new rule here in the office is no pant suits for women, skirts only. He even frowns on some of the ties that men wear. And the men can't leave their office without their coats on. And no one from the production areas can go above the second floor here in the headquarters building without a special badge. To top it off, he gave everyone a little book called 'New Work Habits for a Changing World'."

"Our new president is a piece of work. He required all of us to get 'principled' through this consultant's training program. Then he preaches the information at every meeting. Yet, on day-to-day operations he does not follow one thing that was taught. How can you believe in someone like that?"

"Everyone is now talking about becoming 'principled'. But that is the problem. They are all just talking about it. Then they do little things to make you think that something about them is changing, but as soon as the pressure is back on they revert back to their old ways. Come to think of it, their new way isn't any better."

Positive Comments:

"I trust the levels of hierarchy because I know that management trusts me in the same way that I trust my own people. It's simple. When everyone knows their job and company objectives, and we have clear strategies, then we can all be free to work out the tactics among ourselves. Trust is not a word that means anything, it is in the actions – including my own."

" I believe that most people trust in management around here. Sure they make some mistakes but they are also willing to admit when they have made a mistake. They don't make excuses or blame others. They just say 'It's my fault' and then move on. And they allow us to make mistakes as long as we learn."

"Management people here are just like everyone else. Sometimes they have some tough decisions but they seem to do things in an appropriate manner and keep the balance between productivity and people."

Freedom from Retribution

Negative Comments:

"There are a few managers in every organization that believe in an eye for an eye and a tooth for a tooth. Revenge and retribution seems to be part of their nature. If you know who they are, and you generally do, then stay out of their way. Or go somewhere else before you get shot."

"Unfortunately retribution does exist here. It normally happens when we lose money on a customer or miss a sales opportunity. Management searches for the scapegoat. If you have you facts and documentation you can generally minimize the impact. If not, you better get your resume updated."

"Retribution only exists if you are low enough in the hierarchy that you can be easily replaced. Management here knows that skills in the electronics field are hard to replace so they normally only focus the negative games on those who have lower skill levels."

"There is retribution, but it is subtle. It is both on sex and race. And management allows it to go on. When will they understand that people need to be recognized for their abilities and not the sex, race or age. That's where all the problems lie. It's discrimination. You can't use all the hot shot training programs when the problem is the individual basic belief system to begin with."

Positive Comments:

"It's funny that you ask me if I've experienced retribution. Because come to think of it, there may have been someone higher in the power structure within this organization that tried to express vindictiveness against me just because they did not like something I did or said. But if you ignore it or simply consider the source it does not happen again because the person does not get the fearful response that they were expecting. Retribution is a fact of life. It happens. But it doesn't happen again if you won't let yourself be terrorized."

"Management does not focus on finding some one to blame. Management focuses on the issue and then takes the time to make sure people have learned from the problem. I don't think the managers are consciously practicing retribution."

"My supervisor does not put up with retribution. It doesn't matter where it is between employees or from someone higher in the organization. It is just not tolerated."

Communication and Feedback about Performance

Negative Comments:

"We waste more time around here filling out performance review forms, getting performance reviews, giving performance reviews, evaluating our co-workers and our boss, than we do getting work done. Is there any research to show that feedback on performance once a year on your service anniversary has ever improved the performance of a corporation? I don't think so. At least I've never seen anything. I do believe in performance feedback, but it comes from doing the job and you know it when you do it if was well done or not. If you have to depend upon someone else to tell you then you do not know your job."

"Management does not communicate well with any group. Every statement has a qualifier in it. You can not get clear direction or understanding when all communications have a qualifier statement. People soon learn not to trust the communications because everything is stated in a way that it can have several different meanings, depending upon the situation."

"Performance is measured by popularity. Having the right clothes, right appearance and using the latest buzz phrases all help get you a better performance appraisal. That's too bad for most of the people around here. They end up chasing the carrot on a stick because of the management style."

136

"It's easy. If you are young, white, male and a WASP, you'll get ahead. If not, you won't. Go ask any vice-president if that is the truth, and he will say it isn't so"

Positive Comments:

"Communication is good when you get the response you wanted. All this talk about better communication and management continuously communicating about communicating – nothing ever changes. Guess what? They did not communicate did they? The managers who are the best communicators seem to spend most of their time listening."

"As I heard one of my co-workers say, 'We don't need any fancy programs as long as we all talk and listen'. And that's right. We are free to go to the source on any information that is needed and that's good enough for everyone."

"Performance appraisals are only good to the extent that you end up with better work performance. If you go through the process and nothing changes then you might as well not do the performance reviews. Fortunately, my supervisor understands that very well. So the performance reviews we get are to the point and do not have a lot of filler in them."

Cooperation Among and Within Work Groups and Teams

Negative Comments:

"Management talks a lot about cooperation among and within workgroups and teams, but when you cut to the chase scene it seems like all they really want is competition; not just with other companies, they want competition with each other. If that is what they want, then lets go for it. They are giving contradictory signals. Someone said 'What you do speaks so loud, I can't hear what you say."

"You can not get cooperation when everyone is jumping to the life raft. You have to play the CYA game here if you want to be employed. As long as management allows this to continue there will never be cooperation within the work group."

"How can you get cooperation when everyone knows that the lowest ranking computer engineer person gets fired every year? The ranking and rating system, which we call ranting and raving, is about to make the survivors paranoid. People do not cooperate with one another in a competitive work environment."

"Our human resource director has now started talking about something new called Emotional Intelligence. What a bunch of pop-psychology nonsense. We may have to take an E.I. test to measure our emotional intelligence. Why is it that human resource people keep jumping on the latest gimmick? Is it them, or headquarters?   Now he acts as if he is making these 'emotional deposits' with you and everyone knows it's phony."

Positive Comments:

"Individual competence in doing one's job is necessary but not sufficient. Cooperation occurs when there is respect and dignity and trust. That begins at the top. When we see it at that level it happens at this level. My experience with the managers of this company is that they truly are a team with mutual respect. That's why it works so easily for us."

"Management has developed a feeling of cooperation. Not 100%, but most of the time. The objectives and priorities for the organization are shared with everyone. That way we are all working in the same direction. Since the departments are not competing, cooperation comes easily."

"We used to have a terrible problem around here with cooperation. But once everyone stopped having their turf battles that all changed. You know, it all stopped when we got a new operations manager who believed that we are all working for the same company."

Freedom from Favoritism and Discrimination

Negative Comments:

"Favoritism happens when some managers disagree with policy and consciously violate it. They think they are above the law, so to speak. When top management lets that go on, or is unaware, we all end up suffering in one way or another. And that happens here."

"When problems arise here, it often seems that management hides in hopes that the problem will go away. But it doesn't. That lack of dealing with issues has caused people to believe that discrimination exists. Management can blame no one but itself."

"Everyone likes to make a decent living. Our operations teams make a great living. But it is at people's expense. They are all so afraid of losing their jobs that they play favorites for their own job security. As long as you have something they need, you are a favorite. If not, then they can't remember your name."

Positive Comments:

"One of the issues that every organization has is discrimination. Some people confuse that with prejudice. The management here has made the difference clear to everyone. When they called us all together and said 'If you want to be prejudiced toward some group or individual, then that is your problem. But if you say it out loud or you act it out upon someone, then you are not going to be working here any longer'. That pretty much put a stop to it."

"There is not a real problem here. Sure you do hear of something happening occasionally but it is not very often. And when it does, the supervisors take care of it right away. People get educated in what constitutes discrimination. Basically it is just common sense."

"You can not let some favoritism bother you. We all have our tendencies. You just can't let it get in the way of having a good working environment. If any favoritism bothers a person they will not like working in any organization. Fortunately there is very little here and it's not a concern to people."

Having a Positive Outlook for the Future

Negative Comments:

"Well, to tell you the truth I have a very negative outlook for the future and let me tell you why. We not only have a high throughput of product; we have a high throughput of management. If they don't do well they get fired or retired early or leave to 'pursue other interests'. If they do well, they get transferred to another part of the company. Managers keep coming in to make a positive change, but when each change is based upon theories or short-term focus, then we can't have a good outlook for the future. That's why I keep my options open and my resume up to date."

"We are in the telecommunications industry. How can I have a positive outlook for the future when our turnover rate is nearly 200%? Management sees the problem but does nothing about it. You can not build a strong organization when you have that kind of turnover. You need talented people and people with some dedication. Management thinks it's because of the labor shortage, but reality is that we are not hiring people who are right for the jobs we have to offer. I'm concerned and probably won't stay either."

"The entire focus of this management group is on the quarterly report. It's to a point that they are having weekly updates of financial information to project how the quarter will look. I understand the importance of profit and our investors but how can you have a positive outlook when everything is focused on tomorrow and not long term?"

Positive Comments:

"Managers come and go around here but that's the way it is. But there is one thing that holds this place together and gives us consistent direction. It is our very clearly and simply stated objectives, and that don't change. And we also have clear comprehensible strategies for pursuing those objectives, and they don't change very often either. So when one manager leaves and another one arrives, the style of leadership may be slightly different, but as long as the objectives and strategies remain constant, it does not make that much difference if they change the tactics."

"This is a good organization. We stay focused on our core business and that never changes. As you look over the last ten years we have had a steady increase in business and an expanding customer base. When new people are hired, they are educated in our long-term focus. That way everyone knows why we are here and you can concentrate on doing what you were hired to do."

"We do not get side tracked with all the programs on the market. That stuff may be nice for some people, but it doesn't seem to help the organization long term. Our management group recognizes that window dressing does not add value to the organization."

Opportunities to Use Skills and Abilities

Negative Comments:

"Every since we got the new manager, she has asked us all to write new job descriptions. Then we are all going to be assessed and tested to see who has what skills. Then what's next will be rearranging all of us into narrowly defined roles. Looks like we'll have to learn more and more about less and less. It's the corporation's version of a frontal lobotomy. That looks like the way it is going and if it does, I'm gone."

"We used to help one another and you could use your expertise in numerous areas within the organization. Then someone got the bright idea of creating product specialty centers within the organization and decided each product would be its own little P&L center. Now you are highly restricted on what you can work on. It's no longer enjoyable or a challenge. You don't learn new things like in the past. If it continues, I'll have to seriously consider looking for a job outside the organization."

"We hired people because of their willingness to contribute to the organization. Then our new CEO decided that skills could get outdated as the organization changes. Instead of an environment where you have continuous learning, we now have an environment where people are fired after their expertise in computer programming has been used for the task at hand. I can not survive in this type of work environment. We get our brain cells deleted and then we are sent to the scrap heap along with the old computers."

Positive Comments:

"I know we have job descriptions because we have to had them for ISO 9000. Other than getting that certification our management pays no attention to them. We have few job titles and they are generic. So if someone has some particular skills, or wants to add to their skills, you can,"

"It does not make any difference if you made a mistake. For example, if I screw up, all my boss ever says is 'So what did you learn'? That makes for a great environment. I am not afraid to take calculated risks and my decision making skills are improving over time."

"We have been divided into business units by specific product groups. This has been helpful to the organization. We all work on 3 to 5 different related products at one time. And since we are like a mini-company you get to learn about the marketing, accounting, production, etc. It's an excellent opportunity to learn and grow."

Fair and Equitable Compensation

Negative Comments:

"There are a lot of changes in the pay system. You hear about broad banding, pay for performance, gainsharing, incentive plans – it all comes down to one thing. If I do not believe that I am paid fairly for the work that I'm doing, then I'm not paid fairly for the work I'm doing. Human Resources can have all of its fun and games but it all comes down to being paid fairly for the work that I do. What I do find particularly amusing is all these manipulative games that management plays. They throw money at every problem even when money is not the problem."

"I know if I am paid fairly or not. I just ask others in my profession or call some of my recruiter friends. If I can only get about a 10% difference by changing jobs, then I believe that my pay is fair. If the difference is greater than 10%, then it's time to move on, assuming the new company has freedom to learn new things. When I last spoke to my supervisor about the fact that I am not paid fairly, she tried to explain the program to me. When she doesn't understand it and can't explain it, why should I trust her or the system? Simple, concise facts speak the loudest."

"Management has put too much pay 'at risk'. They tell you how you are being paid fairly, if you hit all the targets, but the truth is that our base rates as compared to other similar jobs is almost 35% below the norm. I do not mind having an 'at risk' portion to my pay. But for fairness, the base rate has to be reasonably close to the norm for my occupation. The 'at risk' portion does not count for home loans, car loans or any other long term credit application. So it does not do me any good for long term investments."

Positive Comments:

"We have a very simple straight forward, easy to understand pay system here. You know where you fit in the survey, and how you fit in the pay range. You know when raise time comes, and you know that you do not have to compete for a small piece of the budget. You get paid for what you do, not what someone else did or did not do. When I am paid fairly, it is neither a negative nor a positive. It's a non-event so that I can do my job without distraction."

"The system we have here is a good system. The supervisor can explain the program and everyone understands it. In fact, human resources has put the program on-line so that any one with questions can get the answers to the questions almost immediately. There is no guess work on where you stand."

"Management has not tried all the new programs around here. I don't think they need to. They reward effort and performance. They fire the dead weight. They don't tolerate discrimination. They listen to people's ideas. Sure they make a mistake now and then. But they will admit it. They are just good honest people like the rest of us and act in an appropriate manner for the situation."

144

Closing the We/They Gap

The recommended strategy for closing the gaps identified by the CVR Employee Attitude Survey Process is for individual managers to adapt their personal leadership styles and communication tactics to the Value Systems found within the workforce.

Adaptation and flexibility does **not** mean that the managers must change their value systems. To close the gap, each manager must adapt his or her leadership style to individual's and/or group's "follower-ship" style.

Communication that will reach all value systems requires differently styled messages — each message targeted to the values present in the workforce.

With sufficient comprehension of value systems, this is not an impossible task, but it requires System 7 Conscious thinking. It is an interesting existential challenge.

Note of Caution: Attempts to introduce gap closers while gap openers remain will result in a net of zero change. The recommended approach is to first eliminate the negative gap openers, before attempting to introduce positive gap closers.

A series of specific tactics for each of the eight factors and each of the six value systems follows.

Trust Among Levels of Hierarchy

Clannish Values Gap Openers

- Fanciful vision and mission statements promulgated by upper management
- Leadership expresses their own distrust of other company management.
- Management which does not follow its own rules
- Visible executive privileges

Clannish Values Gap Closers

- Benevolent and protective supervision and leadership
- Consistent application of procedures and   rules
- Gradual change processes
- Supervisors who are knowledgeable about operations

Cynical Values Gap Openers

- Participative management styles
- Loosely structured employee involvement indecisive leader ship styles.
- "Soft" leadership styles

Cynical Values Gap Closers

- Strong, clear and insistent leadership
- Clear boundaries establishing norms of acceptable behavior
- Consistent leadership
- Tough leadership styles with no tolerance for deviation

Conventional Values Gap Openers

- Constant change of management and supervisory personnel
- Chaotic management styles
- Inconsistent rule applications
- Inconsistent actions

Conventional Values Gap Closers

- Classical and traditional chain of command
- Clear organizational structure and charts indicating the chain-of-command
- Clearly defined plans
- Change introduced on an incremental basis – one step at a time.

Competitive Values Gap Openers

- Few opportunities for exposure to upper management
- Lack of personal achievement awards from upper management
- Lack of recognition for results
- Stringent rules and guidelines by management

Competitive Values Gap Closers

- Opportunities for extensive exposure to the objectives
- Opportunities to demonstrate skills and abilities
- Competitive programs with prizes
- Work environment that allows flexibility under guidelines

Compassionate Values Gap Openers

- Extravagant displays of greed and self-aggrandizement
- Visible signs of executive privilege (company cars, etc.)

- Leadership without compassion for people
- Leadership without concern for community or environment

Compassionate Values Gap Closers

- Corporate support of community and environmental concerns
- Leadership that promotes group harmony
- Leadership which promotes well-being of "total" person
- Tolerance and support for differences in individuals

Conscious Values Gap Openers

- Micro management of tactics by upper management
- No accountability placed on individuals
- Disparity of mission statements and management actions
- Focus on short term results

Conscious Values Gap Closers

- Opportunities to comprehend key organizational strategies
- Execution of tactics without micro-management techniques
- An environment of continuous learning
- No use of reward and punishment systems for motivation

Freedom from Retribution

Clannish Values Gap Openers

- Avoidance, reduction or delay of personal contact by the supervisor
- Inconsistent application of rules on bidding process
- Punishment for utilizing company programs
- Lack of listening skills on personal issues

Clannish Values Gap Closers

- Immediate but gentle feedback on all forms of behavior
- Consistently matching actions with spoken words
- Responsive listening
- Protection from conflict with other internal groups

Cynical Values Gap Openers

- Lack of strong, swift, decisive follow through on the part of management
- Only providing strong negative feedback
- Lack of personal contact on an infrequent basis
- Avoidance of the individual

Cynical Values Gap Closers

- Strong leadership that demonstrates the consequences for good and bad behavior
- Forceful leadership that demonstrates the right way to get things done
- Occasional positive feedback
- Personal recognition of good behavior and work

Conventional Values Gap Openers

- Strong legal disclaimers in handbooks and benefit programs
- Lack of clear documentation of rules, policies and procedures
- Broad statements that do not clearly define desired outcome
- Continual exceptions to written rules

Conventional Values Gap Closers

- Clear, written, consistently applied polices and rules
- Documented procedures for change
- Standard forms of communication (both written and verbal)
- Thorough training

Competitive Values Gap Openers

- Coercion into commitment to impossible goals
- Changing standards after the "game" has started
- Closing the rules to forbid "game" playing
- Lack of consideration for unusual circumstances

Competitive Values Gap Closers

- Employment contracts or "parachutes"
- Positive reinforcement for speaking openly and honestly
- Consideration of the whole picture when goals not met
- Inclusion in management activities

Compassionate Values Gap Openers

- Ridicule for expressing concern over others well being
- Singling out individual mistakes
- Speaking out over safety or environmental concerns
- Punishment for attempting to help less fortunate on company time

Compassionate Values Gap Closers

- Acceptance and support for efforts to improve situations for others
- Encouragement to address safety and environmental issues
- Positive recognition for the group in assisting others
- Group recognition or discipline for actions

Conscious Values Gap Openers

- Recriminations after being encouraged to speak candidly
- Motivation through fear of punishment
- Inconsistent management behavior
- Over reaction by management to undesirable outcomes

Conscious Values Gap Closers

- Alternatives for positions within the company
- Opportunities for speak out on inconsistencies
- No tolerance for discrimination
- Management action is appropriate for the situation

Communication and Feedback about Performance

Clannish Values Gap Openers

- Delayed personal spoken words for the immediate supervisor
- Imbalance of positive and negative feedback
- Lack of supervisory knowledge of work performed
- Only giving written feedback

Clannish Values Gap Closers

- Immediate positive feedback
- Giving oral feedback followed by written documentation
- Information always timely from supervisor
- Information that is useful today and a short time in the future

Cynical Values Gap Openers

- Delay of feedback on positive or negative
- Feedback from people other than supervisor
- No chance to ask questions
- No explanation on how information affects him/her personally

Cynical Values Gap Closers

- Immediate, decisive, exuberant feedback, whether positive or negative
- Constant feedback from supervisor
- Oral communications with some written
- No evasive, very clear answers to questions

Conventional Values Gap Openers

- Failure to document decisions and changes
- Failure to document performance evaluations
- Lack of thoughtfulness and thoroughness
- Differing sets of policies for different parts of the organization

Conventional Values Gap Closers

- Communication and evaluation in a detailed written form "for the record"
- Clearly defined and detailed plans for getting from point A to point B
- Opportunity to provide unrestricted questions and feedback to management
- Management admitting when they are wrong

Competitive Values Gap Openers

- No rewards or trophies
- No recognition for work accomplished
- No competition in the work environment
- Too much negative feedback

Competitive Values Gap Closers

- Public recognition for out performing competition
- Opportunity to publicly talk about or show accomplishments
- An open playing field guided only by boundaries from supervisor
- Over use of positive recognition

Compassionate Values Gap Openers

- Judgmental feedback, which fails to separate the individual from the individual's behavior

- Feedback that is viewed as a manipulative control technique
- Feedback about the individual rather than the group
- Feedback that doesn't consider personal feelings and emotions

Compassionate Values Gap Closers

- Acceptance and forgiveness for errors from peers and coworkers
- Feedback that recognizes group performance
- Open discussions that allow talking about feelings
- Feedback that is not just profit or company oriented

Conscious Values Gap Openers

- Being judged by leaders who are deemed to be incompetent
- Superficial sounding comments that are generic in nature
- Motivating performance through competitive programs
- Untimely or incomplete communications

Conscious Values Gap Closers

- Opportunities for learning from mistakes without rewards or punishments
- Intolerance of poor performance
- Opportunity to participate in decision process
- Quiet, but direct recognition for good performance

Cooperation Among and Within Work Groups and Teams

Clannish Values Gap Openers

- Group leader or supervisor makes disparaging comments about other teams
- Group leaders encouraging competition between work groups
- Systems that have winner and losers between and among work groups
- Lack of supervision showing cooperation

Clannish Values Gap Closers

- Leaders of the work groups demonstrate cooperation and respect for each other
- Cooperation rewarded through positive feedback to group
- Groups encouraged to help each other when necessary
- Systems which foster cooperation rather than competition

Cynical Values Gap Openers

- Management tolerates vindictive behavior
- Management overlooks personal cooperative efforts
- Management focus is on group cooperation without recognizing the individual
- Lack of cooperation is tolerated and sometimes encouraged

Cynical Values Gap Closers

- Management does not accept deviation from set standards of conduct
- Management is paying close attention to everything the person is doing
- Systems that personally reward or recognize proper behavior
- Everyone is held to the same standards

Conventional Values Gap Openers

- A lack of clearly defined roles and responsibilities for individuals and workgroups
- Unclear definition lacking on boundaries, roles and responsibilities
- Inconsistent company wide expectations or goals
- Lack of demonstrated management cooperation

Conventional Values Gap Closers

- Clearly defined procedures, processes, expectations, roles and responsibilities
- No deviation from the written documents
- Management sets the acceptable standards through actions
- Cooperation is measured and judged by supervision

Competitive Values Gap Openers

- No payoff for cooperation
- Cooperation may lower their personal performance rating
- Cooperation does not allow for personal achievements
- System does not allow for some deviations

Competitive Values Gap Closers

- Compete with other teams to see which team can be the most cooperative
- Cooperation does not detract from personal achievement
- Rewards are given for cooperation
- Cooperation is required for advancement

Compassionate Values Gap Openers

- Use of competitive war and football analogies

- Use of programs promoting winners and losers
- Lack of concern for individuals when developing cooperation
- Lack of personal differences in encouraging cooperation

Compassionate Values Gap Closers

- Opportunity and permission to assist others within the group or other groups
- Everybody is considered a winner when cooperation is encouraged
- Systems that recognize personal differences in cooperation
- Management demonstrates cooperation and never discourages cooperation

Conscious Values Gap Openers

- Management preaches teamwork and cooperation while engaging in competition
- Management only interested in cooperation when it is convenient
- Company policies which are inconsistent when cooperative behavior
- The definition of cooperation is associated with 'What's in it for me?'

Conscious Values Gap Closers

- Management demonstrates team behavior
- Management downplays recognition for individuals
- Management is looking out for the good of the organization through cooperation
- The level of cooperation is appropriate for the situation

Freedom from Favoritism and Discrimination

Clannish Values Gap Openers

- There are no people of similar ethnic, sex, etc. representing one's 'tribe'.
- No management or supervisory personnel of same sex or race
- Negative comments by supervision regarding other 'groups'
- Actions which create appearance of favoritism or discrimination

Clannish Values Gap Closers

- Leadership of the organization has a proportional representation
- Management demonstrates a lack of favoritism
- Little opportunity for reversed bias.
- Supervisors do not tolerate any discriminatory comments

Cynical Values Gap Openers

- Lack of listening
- Lack of immediate response
- Openly showing favoritism without cause
- Management taking advantage of their position within organization

Cynical Values Gap Closers

- Management listens to all comments
- Management responds in a quick decisive manner to comments
- No tolerance and immediate punishment for discrimination
- Consistent practices to eliminate favoritism

Conventional Values Gap Openers

- Management does not follow the rules
- Management violates or disregards federal, state or local regulations
- Engagement in affirmative action when there has been no violation of the law
- Company rules or policies appear to favor any groups

Conventional Values Gap Closers

- Management lives up to the spirit of the law
- Management follows its own rules
- Corrective action is used when rules are violated
- Consistency to written rules for all is enforced

Competitive Values Gap Openers

- Giving an advantage to others
- Reversed discrimination are considered as favoritism
- Perquisites provided to one group and not their own group
- When the goals of the game change after the game had started

Competitive Values Gap Closers

- Top management accepting logical excuses for not meeting targets
- No preference shown to any group in a competitive situation
- No special consideration or favors to any group
- No inconsistency where complaints about winners are raised

Compassionate Values Gap Openers

- Any comments or actions that emphasize one group having preferred status to another
- Any visible signs that one group is favored
- Any actions which appear to not give individual respect for differences
- Any policies which restrict the opportunity for groups and individuals to be different

Compassionate Values Gap Closers

- No forms of preferred status for any group, including the top management group.
- Vision and mission statements are fully met by management
- Management admits all wrong decisions and inappropriate actions
- Management gives disadvantaged individuals or groups a "head start"

Conscious Values Gap Openers

- Programs are given lip service
- Management does not follow their rules
- Management does not follow their own vision and mission statements
- Special considerations to create preferential treatment

Conscious Values Gap Closers

- Evidence that the organization is making progress to minimize favoritism
- Evidence that the company is not involved in discriminatory practices
- Management actions are consistent with policy intent
- Consistent and appropriate administration of policies and procedures

Having a Positive Outlook for the Future

Clannish Values Gap Openers

- Requiring a career development plan
- Training that does not relate to the immediate job creates
- Complicated communications and other programs
- Loss of feeling of paternalistic organization

Clannish Values Gap Closers

- On the job training that is relevant
- Providing employment where retiring is possible
- Providing enough money and benefits to provide basic family needs
- Maintain simplicity in programs

Cynical Values Gap Openers

- Required to listen to management talk about long term plans
- Not providing opportunities for individual monetary rewards
- Forced involvement in long term projects
- Training in plans that are not immediately useful

Cynical Values Gap Closers

- Only doing tasks that have a short-term payoff
- Opportunity for more money and short term benefits
- Focus on immediate results
- Management that is concerned about the actions of today only

Conventional Values Gap Openers

- Break down of structure through downsizing and restructuring
- Changes in programs that are based upon management's divine right
- Chaos from unclear direction
- Elimination of processes which maintain order and consistency.

Conventional Values Gap Closers

- Guarantees are in writing such as a handbook
- Seniority is considered important and recognized
- Loyalty is be appreciated and recognized.
- The track record is consistently applied to the future

Competitive Values Gap Openers

- Flat organizational structures
- Downsizing activities
- Hiring extensively from the outside
- Slow organizational growth rate
- Blocked upward mobility by a long term incumbent

Competitive Values Gap Closers

- Current credentials are viewed favorably by the current employer
- Training and skills are marketable to other employers
- Merit is recognized and seniority is discounted
- When key executives show unbounded enthusiasm for continuous growth

Compassionate Values Gap Openers

- Reduction in the employment level
- No assistance for those losing their jobs

- The perception of continued injustices to others
- Exploitation by management in terms of not sharing increased profits

Compassionate Values Gap Closers

- Management that is ethical and caring
- Management that adopts the community as part of an extended company family
- Management which gives time and money to societal causes
- Management that shows forgiveness to all for the long term

Conscious Values Gap Openers

- Management disregard for logical improvements
- Over reaction to market conditions
- Management acting as if the vision statement will actually be realized
- Lack of planning for future products and investment for growth

Conscious Values Gap Closers

- Management is concerned about the direction the organization is going
- Management is not focused upon fixed objectives.
- Demonstrated improvements in key business areas
- Sincere attempts by management to make non-selfish improvements

Opportunities to Use Skills and Abilities

Clannish Values Gap Openers

- Requirements to perform multiple task and skills outside of basic job requirements
- Programs that endorse multi-skill concepts
- Rotational job assignments
- Flexible work structure

Clannish Values Gap Closers

- Encouragement to methodically learn new skills and abilities
- Slow, extensive on-the-job training by a competent supervisor
- Participation in problem solving process by using job knowledge
- Recognition for attaining skill levels

Cynical Values Gap Openers

- Expectation to do more work without more money
- Expectation to perform work that is outside the job classification
- Expectations for perfection
- Too close of scrutiny by supervision

Cynical Values Gap Closers

- Personal recognition for clear demonstrated skills
- The acquisition of skills results in more money
- Trust from supervision that the job will get done right
- Tolerance for some imperfection

Conventional Values Gap Openers

- Not recognizing or utilizing skills that people already possess
- Not recognizing the knowledge that people already possess
- Multi-skilled requirements without written criteria
- No objective assessment of criteria and skills

Conventional Values Gap Closers

- Recognizing the skills and knowledge that they have already acquired
- Encouragement to use all acquired skills and knowledge
- Objective measurements for skill development
- Clear, concise, written plans for skill and knowledge development

Competitive Values Gap Openers

- Work environments where actions are valued more than the results
- Imposed restrictions on ethics and budgets
- Rigidly enforced rules and procedures
- Specialization to a point of slowing the personal process of success

Competitive Values Gap Closers

- Risk taking that is honestly rewarded and recognized
- People allowed their 'bragging rights'
- Good results are put on public display as a job well done
- Cross-training for personal advancement and benefit

Compassionate Values Gap Openers

- Classification or labeling of people
- No recognition of the whole human being as a person
- Programming of people

- Forcing there is only one right way to complete a task

Compassionate Values Gap Closers

- People are allowed to pursue their goals
- The risk of negative judgement is minimal.
- Acceptance of skills of all types whether work related or not
- Opportunities to be creative outside of current job assignments

Conscious Values Gap Openers

- Constriction of freedom
- Compartmentalized jobs according to their ability for short term financial payoff
- Exploitation by management
- No opportunity to learn

Conscious Values Gap Closers

- Opportunity to learn from incomplete skills and abilities
- Failure to always perform perfectly is accepted as a natural human condition
- Encouragement of involvement in new areas
- Recognition as skills are improving

Fair and Equitable Compensation

Clannish Values Gap Openers

- Variable pay plans
- Piece rate systems
- Merit progression
- Individual bonuses

Clannish Values Gap Closers

- Automatic progressions
- Group bonuses
- Service premiums
- Cost of living raises

Cynical Values Gap Openers

- Automatic progressions
- Group bonuses
- Service premiums
- Seniority pay

Cynical Values Gap Closers

- Individual bonuses
- Individually merit raises
- Piece rates
- Merit pay programs

Conventional Values Gap Openers

- Individual competition
- Pay for performance in a competitive mode

- Merit programs
- Programs where criteria are not controllable

Conventional Values Gap Closers

- Automatic progression
- Service premiums
- Share and share alike bonuses
- Some progression (such as skill) if there is an objective way of measuring skills

Competitive Values Gap Openers

- Automatic progression
- Service premiums
- Seniority based pay
- Equal shared group bonuses

Competitive Values Gap Closers

- Pay for performance (%)
- Competitive rating systems
- Individually determined bonuses
- Pay for the acquisition of skills

Compassionate Values Gap Openers

- Pay for performance
- Competitive rating systems
- Individual payments to star performers
- Individual pay for skill

Compassionate Values Gap Closers

- Automatic progressions

- Group bonuses with same dollars for all
- Service premiums
- Versatility premiums

Conscious Values Gap Openers

- Not paid fairly for the work that is being performed
- Using the pay system as punishment or reward
- Competitive practices that reward game playing
- Compensation that focuses on short term accomplishments only

Conscious Values Gap Closers

- Pay must be comparable to others for the skills involved.
- The system is not important but the result is very important.
- Focus on contribution, not bell-shaped curves
- Maintaining a balance in all programs

Final Comments

Closing the we/they gap will aid in fulfilling corporate vision and values statements.

Closing the we/they gap will aid in maintaining or attaining a unionfree status.

Closing the we/they gap will aid continuous quality improvement efforts.

Closing the we/they gap will improve the attitudes of employees, regardless of their value systems.

Closing the we/they gap requires communicating management's objectives in language compatible with the value systems of all employees.

Closing the we/they gap will occur with this strategy:

First, eliminate the negatives
then,
accentuate the positives.

Terminology

Management Fad: A modern day consultant technique that creates compulsive enthusiasm, interest and a craze for a short period of time. Has no organizational long term lasting effect or value.

Management Fashion: The overwhelming surge to conform to the style, manners and language of the most current predictors of business trends, best selling authors and business overlords.

Management Folderol: Actions and ideas that are showy but worthless. Normally viewed as trite, trinket, bauble and mere nonsense. Truly gewgaw in nature.

CVR is an employee relations consulting group that began in 1974 and has worked with over 3000 organizations in every field of endeavor, both unionfree and unionized. Our approach is not anti-union, nor is it pro-management, nor even pro-employee. We simply believe that conflict is unnecessary and unwarranted when concern for people and concern for productivity are blended synergistically. Our surveys and workshops help to bring the values of employees and the goals of management into systematic alignment.

Contact **CVR** at:

8848 Greenville Avenue
Dallas, TX 75243

Phone: 214-553-8848
Fax: 214-553-9191
E-mail: cvr@alitnet.net or
www.cvrdallas.com